Wings of Cessna

Model 120 to the Citation III

Edward H. Phillips

To Bob Francis
Happy Flying in a Cessna!
Edward H. Phillips
9-15-90

FLYING BOOKS
1401 Kings Wood Road
Eagan, Minnesota 55122

DEDICATION

Airplanes are not living things, yet they are conceived in the minds of men, shaped by the eye and wrought from the labor of human hands. For more than half a century the men and women of Cessna have made aluminum and steel come to life and take wing. Thousands of people, from the president to the production line worker, have contributed their unique talents and abilities to make Cessna the world's largest producer of light airplanes.

Credit for this success has been given, quite deservedly, to former President/Chairman of the Board Dwane L. Wallace and his carefully chosen staff. But it wasn't leadership alone that put the company on top...the real reason was its corps of extremely dedicated, hard working employees, men and women who got the job done.

Men like Ray Richards, who compiled cost estimates for government contract proposals; Don Hammer, whose extensive knowledge of financial matters at hundreds of Cessna dealers permitted solid credit decisions; Wayne Hess, cost estimating supervisor, responsible for calculating unit costs for nearly a hundred thousand parts in inventory; Warren "Scritch" Scritchfield, payroll supervisor, who made sure everyone got paid the right amount 52 times a year.

Hundreds of equally dedicated employees worked in engineering, manufacturing, tooling, inspection, training and other important departments. Women like Pat Ambler, administrative assistant to the corporate comptroller, perhaps the hardest working employee Cessna ever had; Merna Cherrett, quality assurance department, who processed paperwork to license over 100,000 airplanes.

It was people like "Muggs" Sowers, Military Service Manager, that kept hundreds of military Cessnas flying around the world, and the unsung heros like Bob Chalfant, often roused from sleep to track down one errant ELT among 500 factory-fresh airplanes on Cessna Field.

These employees, and many just like them, performed a multitude of mundane, thankless tasks that were vital to the everyday operation of an aircraft company like Cessna. Perhaps Dwane Wallace summed it up best when he called them all "the glue that holds the company together."

To the thousands of Cessnans, past, present and future, who perform their jobs with pride and that unique sense of accomplishment that comes only from building flying machines, "The Wings Of Cessna" is respectfully dedicated to you.

Copyright © 1986 Flying Books, Publishers & Wholesalers, 1401 Kings Wood Road, Eagan, Minnesota 55122

Library of Congress Cataloging in Publication Data

Phillips, Edward H.

Wings of Cessna
Model 120 to the Citation III

86-72359

ISBN 0-911139-05-2

All rights reserved. No part of this book may be reproduced in any form without the permission of the publisher.

Printed in the United States of America. First edition.

THE WINGS OF CESSNA
Model 120 to the Citation III
An Illustrated History

Edward H. Phillips

Of all the light airplanes built in America since the 1930s, the Cessna series of monoplanes has emerged as one of the best known today to both airman and layman alike, spreading their wings to serve the needs of flight training, charter, corporate, private, agricultural and military aviation for over 50 years. The purpose of this book is to illustrate the Cessna airplanes built from 1946 through 1986 in a pictorial format, one that lends itself to the interests of the weekend pilot as well as the aero historian. In the half century since the Model C-34 took flight and ushered the company into its second era, six basic families of airplanes were created, designed to cover a wide spectrum of the general aviation marketplace. Each series of airplanes are presented as follows:

100 series, single-engine: Model 120, 140, 150, 152, 160, 170, 172, 175, 180, 182, 185, 187, 188, 190, 195.

200 series, single-engine: Model 205, 206, 207, 208, 210.

300 series, single-engine: Model 305, 308, 309, 319, 325; multi-engine piston: Model 303, T303, 310, 320, 335, 340.

400 series, multi-engine piston: 401, 402, 404, 411, 414, 421; multi-engine turbine: 406, 425, 441

500 series, multi-engine turbine: 500, 501, 550, 551, 552

600 series, multi-engine turbine: 650

In addition, information is included regarding experimental models that were built and flown, but because of flight performance, economic or market considerations were not given production status. The reader will find information conveniently grouped for each model and its derivative that pertains to year of introduction, price, quantity produced and general specifications. When applicable, additional information on a specific model or other notes of interest will be included. Appendix A contains footnotes pertaining to certain models and constructor number blocks. Three-view drawings are included with the text for each major single and multi-engine model.

The author wishes to express his appreciation for the ongoing assistance and guidance provided by Bob Pickett, whose knowledge of Cessna's 60-year history coupled with his extensive photographic and written files made this book possible.

Also deserving thanks for their help in procuring Cessna information are Dean Humphrey, Alice Helser, Roger Fife, Tim Brogan, Don Mallonee, Jim McCuen, Larry Wiggins, Jim Hild and Chuck Braden of the Cessna Aircraft Company.

All photographs used in this publication are provided courtesy of the Cessna Aircraft Company and Robert J. Pickett collections except where noted. The author wishes to express his appreciation to Cessna and Mr. Pickett for use of their archival materials.

Edward H. Phillips
Wichita, Kansas
June, 1986

A BRIEF HISTORY OF THE CESSNA AIRCRAFT COMPANY

The name Cessna has been known around the world for over 50 years as a premier manufacturer of light aircraft. It all started with a Kansas farmboy named Clyde Vernon Cessna who taught himself to fly in 1911, was a well-known exhibition pilot by 1918 and, in partnership with Walter Beech and Lloyd Stearman formed the Travel Air Manufacturing Company, Inc. in 1925.

Never satisfied with biplanes, Cessna believed that full-cantilever monoplanes were the only practical design for an airplane and built the three-seat "Phantom" as a flying prototype in August, 1927, forming a partnership with Victor Roos of Omaha, Nebraska as the Cessna-Roos Aircraft Company.

The alliance was short-lived, however, with Roos resigning in December and the firm's title reverting to the Cessna Aircraft Company as it is today. Despite sound designs and excellent performance on moderate horsepower, Cessna only built about 250 airplanes from 1927 through 1931, when the Depression forced closure of the factory.

Undaunted, Cessna and his son Eldon formed a partnership in concert with a small group of supporters and built four airplanes in 1932-33, being a totally separate entity from the original company. The CR-1 racer prototype was rebuilt into the CR-2/CR-2A, and famed racing pilot Johnny Livingston had the CR-3 custom-built to his requirements. The fourth ship was the C-3 cabin monoplane sold originally to White Castle hamburger king Walter Anderson.

Following the crash of the CR-2A in 1933, which killed pilot Roy Liggett, Clyde Cessna lost much of his enthusiasm for aviation. He never again actively participated in American aeronautics, only reluctantly agreeing to assist nephews Dwane and Dwight Wallace in their quest to reopen the Cessna factory.

Their efforts were successful and in January, 1934 the Cessna Aircraft Company was busy constructing the classic Model C-34, designed by Dwane Wallace, Tom Salter and Jerry Gerteis. Introduced in the middle of the Great Depression, the C-34 sold well. The prototype, c/n 254, NC12599 was flown to victory at Cleveland in 1935 by George Harte, winning the Detroit News Trophy. In 1936 Dwane Wallace took the checkered flag in another C-34 and won permanent possession of the Detroit trophy along with the title "World's Most Efficient Airplane".

The critical need for an advanced trainer found Cessna with huge contracts for a military version of the T-50, known as the "Bobcat" for the Americans and the "Crane I/Ia" for the Royal Canadian Air Force. Over 800 were built for the Canadians and over 4,500 served the U.S. Army and Navy during the war.

When production was halted in 1944, 5,399 airplanes had been built. When peace returned the company was ready for the expected boom in aircraft sales with the rough and ready Model 120/140 series of monoplanes which quickly established themselves as the market leaders from 1946 to 1951.

The Model 190/195 proved to be a favorite mount for the pilot who wanted cabin comfort and high performance, and the advent of the popular Model 170 offered room for four and very respectable cross-country speeds on only 145 hp.

By the 1950s Cessna was intent on expanding their product line into the twin-engine category, starting with the Model 310 of 1953 followed by the Model 320 in 1961. Cessna then introduced the novel, fixed-gear Model 336 with center-line thrust in 1961 that was quickly supplanted by the retractable gear Model 337 in 1965.

Next came the all-new 400 series, with the Model 411 making its debut in 1962, being joined by the Model 401 in 1965, 402 in 1966, 421 in 1967, 414 in 1969 followed later by the Model 404 in the late 1970s.

In 1968 the Cessna Aircraft Company was launched into the jet age when the Fanjet 500 project, later changed to the Cessna 500 Citation, flew in 1969. The Citation was a very successful design for the company and subsequent models soon established Cessna as a leader in the business jet market.

In the late 1970s the company designated a follow-on jet to the Model 500 series with the 650-series Citation III. Using a supercritical airfoil and advanced aerodynamics, the new airplane found ready buyers when introduced in 1982.

During the 1950s and 60s Cessna also expanded their corporate base by purchasing the Aircraft Radio Corporation in February, 1959, giving the company access to the aircraft electronics/avionics market for both commercial and military applications.

One year later Cessna acquired Avions Max Holste in Reims, France, renaming it Reims Aviation in 1962. The European-based factory gave the Wichita company a ready outlet for its products, although slight differences exist between American and French versions of a particular airplane model.

Cessna next turned its attention to the South American market, establishing Cessna Argentina S.A.I.C. at Mendoza, Argentina in October, 1961, opening up the vast reaches of the South American continent to Cessna products. Cessna's affiliate in Colombia also built several light single-engine models.

The McCauley Industrial Corporation of Dayton, Ohio became a subsidiary of Cessna in August of 1960, producing aircraft propellers for reciprocating and turbine-powered aircraft around the world.

In September, 1985 the Cessna Aircraft Company was acquired by General Dynamics, just over 50 years after Dwane and Dwight Wallace resurrected the company from the depths of the Great Depression.

Cessna stands at the threshold of its second half century in aviation, a time of challenge and courage that will find it more than ready to explore new frontiers in aeronautics and aerospace technologies.

SUPPLEMENTARY INFORMATION

Cessna has utilized three domestic factories for the production of its single and multi-engine airplanes. The first (and the oldest) is the Commercial Aircraft Division, located on the original factory site built for Clyde V. Cessna in 1929.

All commercial and military aircraft were designed and built at the East Wichita site, from the C-34 through the early series of the Model 310. As the commercial product line continued to expand in the late 1950s, a new factory was deemed necessary in order to handle the company's increasing military business.

In 1956 Cessna opened its second factory, known as the Military Aircraft Division, adjacent to Wichita's Mid-Continent Airport on the west side of the city. Also known as the Wallace Division in honor of former company president Dwane Wallace, the facility eventually became responsible for design and manufacture of all commercial twin-engine models by the early 1960s, starting with the Model 310F of 1961.

By 1967, Cessna had opened its third factory at Strother Field near Winfield, Kansas, to produce single-engine aircraft, in particular the Model 150/152 and 172/Cutlass RG series.

Cessna has issued consecutive constructor numbers (c/n) for production aircraft since the prototype Model AA of August, 1927, which carried c/n 112. These numbers continued through c/n 591, a Model C-165 that was the last of the famous Airmaster series produced. However, not all c/n were used during this era. For example, c/n 592 through 599 were available but not issued in the Airmaster series.

When the Model T-50 was introduced in late 1939, constructor numbers began at c/n 1000 and continued up to c/n 6700, the final UC-78 "Bobcat" to roll off the assembly line in 1944. It should be noted that not all c/n were used by the company, with many numbers not being utilized (a total of 5,399 Model T-50/AT-17/UC-78-series airplanes were built).

Cessna reserved a block of numbers beginning with c/n 600 through c/n 999 exclusively for experimental designs and these numbers are still used today. When World War II came to an end in 1945 and production of the Model 120/140 began, Cessna soon realized that the original block of numbers (c/n 8000 to 8999) allocated for these models would be insufficient due to the new airplane's booming popularity with postwar flyers.

To overcome this problem, more c/n blocks were authorized and kept up with the blazing pace of sales until the fall of 1947, when production slowed dramatically because the two-place trainer market had virtually filled up.

The Model 190/195 also experienced the need for additional c/n groups. Introduced in 1947, the Model 190/195 were given c/n 7000 to 7999 but high customer acceptance of the new ship demanded further c/n blocks 16000 to 17000 to cope with higher than expected production rates.

During the expansion years of 1954 through 1970, Cessna was slowly realizing its goal of producing an airplane for every need and found that the old system of c/n blocks were becoming ever more complex and cumbersome.

Beginning in 1961 the company initiated use of the particular airplane model number to prefix a series of c/n blocks. For example, the Model 172 c/n became 17248500 or a Model 150 was designated as c/n 15059350. New designs begin with a c/n such as 172RG0001 to designate a new block of constructor numbers.

Recognizing the need to differentiate between single and twin-engine c/n blocks, Cessna created a variation of the 1961 method for its multi-engine models. Each model year has its own distinct c/n group, such as c/n 310H0001 to c/n 310H0148 for the 1963 model year and c/n 310R2101 to c/n 310R2140 for 1981.

Cessna models built in France by Reims Aviation carry a prefix to the c/n, such as c/n F17202195 to easily identify them as Reims-built aircraft. The same procedure is true for all other models like the 150/152; a 1984 152 built by Reims Aviation would be designated F15201944.

Military airplanes like the T-41 version of the basic Model 172 were built within a Model 172 c/n block that was not separated from the commercial 172 numbers. Other military aircraft such as the L-27A (U-3A) and Model 310E (U-3B), M337B (0-2A) and 337A (0-2B) followed a similar procedure.

There were many individual and fleet sales of airplanes to foreign countries that were made under the Military Assistance Program (MAP) and were sold from the normal production line for that model and carried a normal c/n in many cases.

The reader is cautioned that it is often impossible to interpolate when a particular model was built or to determine exact production configuration by examination of c/n blocks exclusively. There are frequent paperwork changes to c/n groups that shift numbers from one model year to another or even one airplane to another.

Cessna, like many other aircraft manufacturers, often eliminates certain c/n or c/n blocks for a specific reason or changes the number sequence, even during the model year. An example would be the 1984 prototype P210N, c/n P21000833.

Cessna built P21000833 as the engineering prototype for the 1984 model year. However, no P210Ns were built in 1984 so the company changed c/n P21000833 to P21000835 and used it as the 1985 model year prototype.

Therefore, the same airplane carried two different c/ns and represented the prototype for two model years, with c/n P2100833 being reflected on paper as never being built.

Another example is the 1984 Model 152. A block of seven c/n were originally destined for 1983 airplanes but were not used, becoming a part of the 1984 model year sequence. As an example, one of these seven numbers was c/n 15285797 for the 1983 model year that was changed to c/n 15285861 for the 1984 year.

With such number manipulations commonplace, it becomes clear that anyone researching a particular c/n must use caution when trying to ascertain precise information, especially at the beginning and end of a model year as well as during the production run.

▲ MODEL 120   ATC A-768   1946-49

First offered by Cessna in 1946, the Model 120 was a two-place, conventional gear cabin monoplane featuring a fabric-covered (aluminum structure) semi-cantilever wing and an all-metal fuselage and empennage assembly. The Model 120-A, with steerable tailwheel and co-pilot brakes, and the Model 120-B, with 120-A equipment plus complete electrical system was offered in May, 1946 but none are known to have been built. 1947 Model 120 featured improved cabin heating/ventilation, stainless steel mufflers, shielded ignition harness, complete cabin upholstery, new control wheels, seats and totally redesigned engine cowling. An electrical system was optional on the Model 120 at extra cost. 1948 120s had the main gear strut angle changed to place the wheels three inches further forward than previous models to improve ground handling. 120 c/n were intermixed with 140 c/n from c/n 8000 to 11846 in 1946. Total built: 2172 (including 1945 prototype) from June, 1946 to May, 1949. Price: May, 1946: $2695, increasing to $2845 in September, 1947. Engine: Continental C-85, 85 hp; gross weight: 1450 pounds; maximum speed: 120 mph; wingspan: 32 feet 10 inches; service ceiling: 15,500 feet.

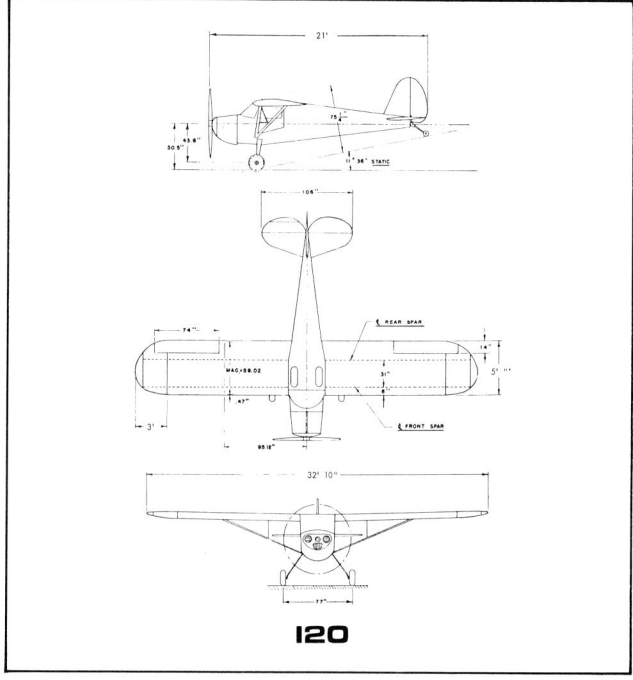

◄ MODEL 140 (PROTOTYPE)   ATC A-768   1945

In anticipation of the post-World War Two flying boom, Cessna engineers designed and developed the Model 140 as an inexpensive trainer/sport airplane. Three prototypes were built, with the second example (c/n 8002, NC41684) illustrated in this view. Wing featured aluminum spars and rib structure but was fabric-covered while the all-metal fuselage was a Cessna first. Spring steel landing gear design was purchased from S.J. Wittman and used on all Model 120/140 ships. First flight was June 28, 1945. Total built: 3. Engine: Continental C-85-12, 85 hp; gross weight: 1450 pounds; maximum speed: 120 mph; wingspan: 32 feet 10 inches; service ceiling: 15,500 feet.

▲ MODEL 140   ATC A-768   1946-49

Cessna's Model 140 included rear cabin windows, complete electrical system and mechanically-operated wing flaps. Intended for the trainer/private owner market, the two-place 140 featured a fabric-covered (aluminum structure) semi-cantilever wing and all-metal fuselage/empennage. Built on the same production line with the Model 120, constructor numbers were consecutive regardless of model type. In 1946, Cessna offered optional radio, propeller hub cover, mixture control, wheel fairings, steerable tailwheel and Grimes landing light as extra equipment when available. The 1947 140 had a mixture control and cigarette lighter as standard equipment. Total built: 4904 (including three prototypes) from May, 1946 to April, 1949. Price: May, 1946: $3245; changes in Continental engine prices forced an increase to $3345 in September, 1947, with another increase to $3385 in 1948/49. The last Model 140 was c/n 15074, manufactured in April of 1949. Engine: Continental C-85-12, 85 hp until 1948 when the C-90-12 of 90 hp was a $200 option; gross weight: 1450 pounds, maximum speed: 120 mph (C-85), 125 mph (C-90); wingspan: 32 feet 10 inches; service ceiling: 15,500 (C-85), 15,600 (C-90).

 (see next page)

Prototype Model 140 instrument panel - 1945. Magneto switch is behind left control wheel, throttle at lower center. ▼

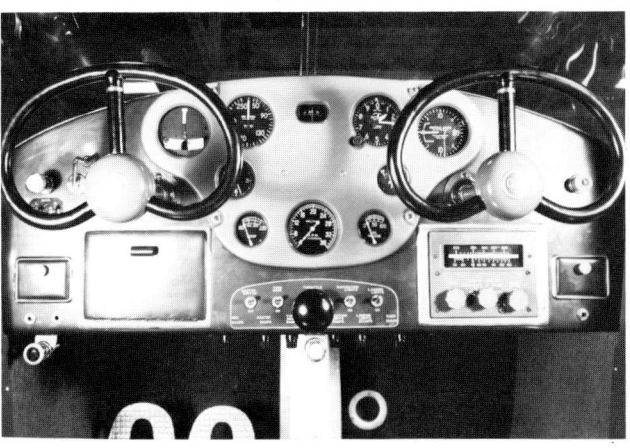

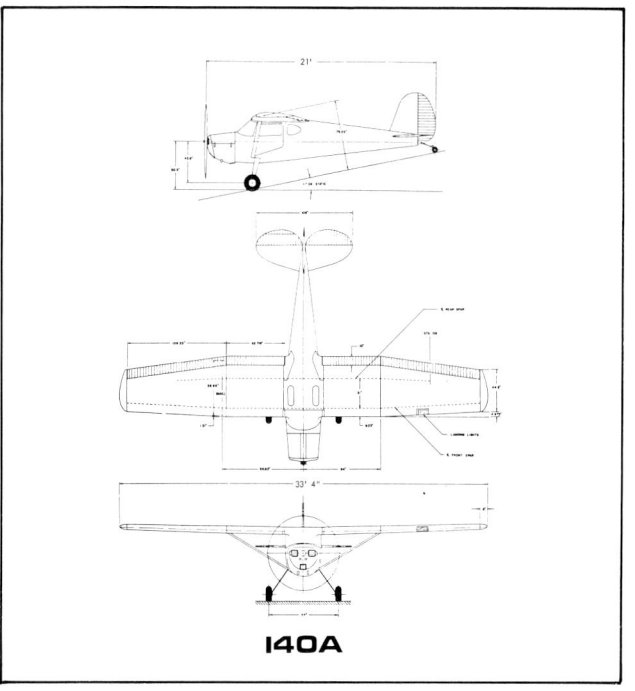

1947 Model 140 interior was spartan but functional. Note cabin roof skylights.

1949 Model 140A instrument panel installed in N2142V, c/n 14367.

◄ MODEL 140A   ATC 5A2   1949

The Model 140 received an all-metal wing in 1949 and became the 140A, with a graceful, tapered outboard planform that improved both appearance and performance. First deliveries occurred in June, 1949, with either the Continental C-85-12 or C-90-12 engine installed until December 5, 1950, when Cessna no longer offered the C-85 powerplant (except for customer-furnished engines). Total built: 1949: 175. Price: $3495 with C-85-12, $3695 with C-90-12 engine. Engine: Continental C-85-12, 85 hp (until December, 1950), then C-90-12, 90 hp; gross weight: 1500 pounds; maximum speed: 125 mph; wingspan: 33 feet four inches; service ceiling: 15,500 (C-85), 15,600 feet (C-90).

▼ MODEL 140A   ATC 5A2   1950-51

Cessna improved the Model 140A in 1950 by introducing larger, softer seat cushions, stiffened cabin doors with improved sealing; the C-85 engine incorporated rubber mount pads used with the C-90 powerplant, anti-slosh baffles were added to the inboard section of the fuel tanks, new window latches were incorporated along with a redesigned parking brake control. Options included dual 21-gallon fuel tanks for increased range, special door windows for enhanced visibility downward on the patroller version, crosswind landing gear, factory-installed avionics (including VOR equipment), a controllable-pitch Beech-Roby propeller on the C-85 engine and overall paint scheme featuring high gloss enamel finish in eight basic colors. A complete set of gyroscopic flight instruments could also be installed, along with an available amber blind flying hood and special blue goggles for the pilot to practice instrument flight. N5320C, shown in this view, has the optional and popular wheel fairings installed along with overall gloss enamel paint scheme. Production of all Model 140As from 1949 to 1951 included c/n 15200 through c/n 15724. Because of growing demand for the larger, faster four-place Model 170, 140A production terminated in March, 1951. Total built: 1950-51: 350; (1949: 175; total Model 140A production: 525; (124 C-85, 401 C-90). Price: With C-85 engine: $3495; with C-90 engine: $3695. Engine: Continental C-85-12, 85 hp or C-90-12, 90 hp; gross weight: 1500 pounds; maximum speed: 125 mph; wingspan: 33 feet four inches; service ceiling: 15,600 feet.

▲   MODEL 150   ATC 3A19   1959

After an eight-year absence from the trainer market, Cessna again put fledglings in the air with the new 1959 Model 150. Originally known as the Model 142 when flown in 1957, the two-place airplane was redesignated 150 in October, 1957. Featuring many proven design/structural concepts of the Model 140A, the 150 sported tri-cycle landing gear, all-metal construction, "Para-Lift" flaps and a new empennage design. Sold as the Standard, Trainer and Commuter versions, the first production ship (c/n 17001, N5501E) is illustrated in a "Standard" paint scheme with optional wheel fairings. 1959 Model 150 production spanned c/n 17001 through 17683 (including the 1957 prototype). Total built (1959): 684. Price: Standard: $6995; Trainer: $7940; Commuter: $8545. Engine: Continental O-200A, 100 hp; gross weight: 1500 pounds; maximum speed: 124 mph; wingspan: 33 feet four inches; service ceiling: 15,300 feet. Model 150 first flight: 9-12-57; pilot: Bill Thompson.

▼   MODEL 150A/B/C   ATC 3A19   1960-63

Cessna continued to improve the Model 150 and by 1962 the 150 featured the larger rear windows, repositioned main landing gear (two inches aft), 12 pound reduction in empty weight and a new instrument panel incorporated in the 1961 150A. New wingtips, a pointed, fiberglass propeller spinner, revised instrument panel denoted the 150B/C changes. Total built: 1960 150: 334; 150A: 333; 150B: 350; 150C: 387. Price: 1962 Commuter: $8995. Engine: Continental O-200A, 100 hp; gross weight: 1500

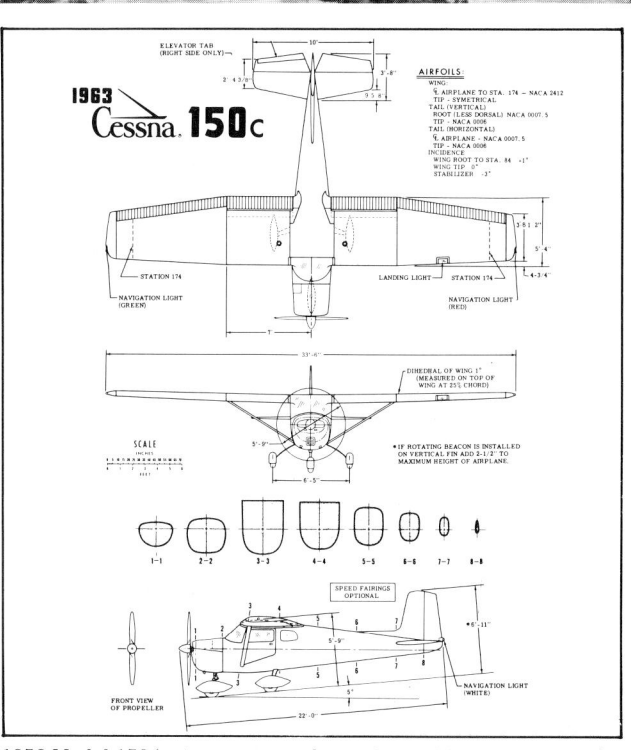

1959 Model 150 instrument panel complete with gyroscopic ▼ flight instruments and Narco Superhomer VHT-3 VHF transceiver.

pounds; maximum speed: 127 mph; wingspan: 33 feet six inches; service ceiling: 15,600 feet (150B).

MODEL 150D   ATC 3A19   1964 ▶

In 1964 the Model 150D ushered in the era of "Omni-Vision" with its large rear window. Gross weight increased to 1600 pounds including a 40 pound useful load boost that was a welcome change as more avionics and instruments were being added to trainers by the mid-1960s. Interior color choices increased to four while 12 exterior colors were available. Airplane illustrated is c/n 644, N5420E, 1964 150D prototype with optional wheel fairings that were redesigned in 1963 (150C) to be interchangeable with other single-engine Cessnas. Total built: 1964: 686; 1963 Model 150C, last year with straight-back fuselage design: 387. Price: Commuter: $9495 (1964). Engine: Continental O-200A, 100 hp; gross weight: 1600 pounds; maximum speed: 125 mph; wingspan: 33 feet six inches; service ceiling: 12,650 feet.

MODEL 150E/F/G   ATC 3A19   1965-67 ▶

Production of the Model 150F for 1966 saw three substantial changes to the series: Cessna's "Flight-Sweep" tail, raked back at a stylish 35 degree angle; larger, wider cabin doors for easier entry/exit with bigger windows; increased baggage area giving a full 24 cubic feet of luggage space. Minor changes were lengthened propeller spinner, electrically operated flaps and interior/exterior colors/appointments, 6.00 x 6.0 wheels and brakes replacing earlier 5.00 x 5.0 type. The 150F was the first 150 built in France (from sub-assemblies shipped from Wichita) by Cessna's affiliate, Reims Aviation. Total built: 1966: 2934; Reims Aviation: 1965 Model 150E: 760; 1966 150F: 67. Price: 1966 Model 150F: $9275 (Commuter). Engine: Continental O-200A, 100 hp (including Reims Aviation Model F150F); gross weight: 1600 pounds; maximum speed: 125 mph; wingspan: 32 feet 8 1/2 inches (length increased to 23 feet 9 inches on the Commuter and 23 feet on the Standard/Trainer versions because of the new swept tail); service ceiling: 12,650 feet. (Reference Appendix A, #1)

MODEL 150H/J/K   ATC 3A19   1968-70 ◀

Cessna delivered the 10,000th Model 150 (a 1968 Model 150H, c/n 15068975, N22124) and redesigned the instrument panel for the 1969 150J version. The 1970 150K incorporated the new panel and added conical (cambered) wing tips on the Commuter version only. Interior changes consisted of a molded headliner, optional skylights and redesigned seat installation for more legroom. The 150K was the last model to use the original spring steel configuration for the main landing gear (A150K Aerobat included). Total built: 1970: Domestic: 875; Reims: 129; 1969 150J: Domestic: 1820; Reims: 140; 1968 150H: Domestic: 2110; Reims: 170. Price: 1970 Model 150K: $11,450. Engine: Continental (Reims-Rolls-Royce) O-200A, 100 hp; gross weight: 1600 pounds; maximum speed: 150K: 122 mph; wingspan: 33 feet two inches (Commuter), 32 feet 8 1/2 inches (Standard/Trainer); service ceiling: 12,650 feet. (Reference Appendix A, #2)

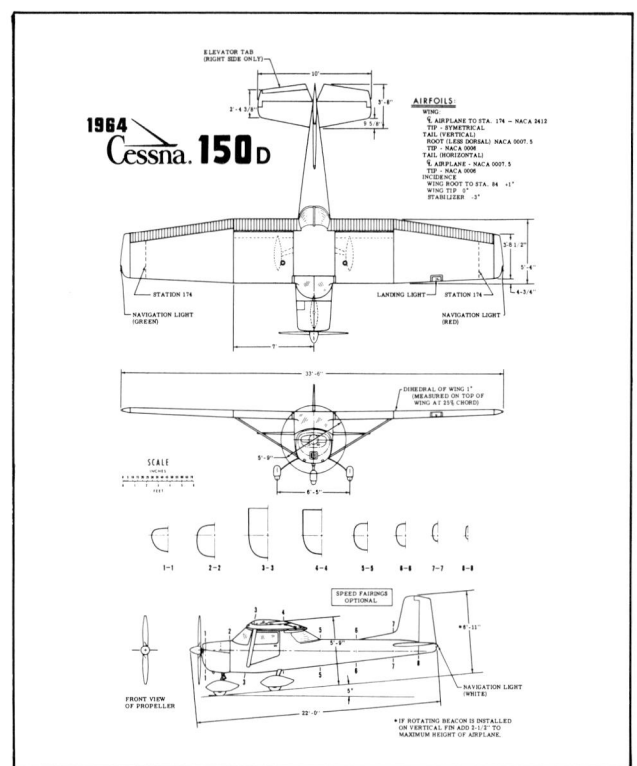

1967 Model 150G instrument panel. Note electric flap control switch on right subpanel, open-view control wheels. ▶

MODEL A150K/L ATC 3A19 1970-74

In 1970 Cessna further expanded the 150's versatility by introducing the A150K "Aerobat", designed for entry-level aerobatic training and certified to +6/-3 G units. The 1974 A150L Aerobat shared improvements made to the 1974 150L models, such as restyled wheel fairings, interior improvements, new paint scheme, optional dual landing/taxi lights located in the engine cowling and optional wing tip strobe lights. A Clark "Y" propeller airfoil increased maximum speed by 4 mph. Powerplant for the Reims FRA150L was the 130 hp Continental (Rolls-Royce) O-240A (originally incorporated on 1972 Reims FRA150L models), marking the first engine change since 1959. Total built: Domestic: 1974: 94; 1973: 84; 1972: 60; 1971: 50; Reims FRA150L: 1974: 50; 1973: 45; 1972: 46; 1971 FA150L: 39. Note: Argentina produced Model A-A150L. Total: 1972: 6; 1973: 3; Price: 1970: $12,000. Engine: Continental (Rolls-Royce) O-200A, 100 hp (A150L series); Continental (Rolls-Royce) O-240A, 130 hp (FRA150L series); gross weight: 1600 pounds (A150L series), 1650 pounds (FRA150L series); maximum speed: 124 mph; wingspan: 32 feet 8 1/2 inches; service ceiling: 14,000 feet. (Reference Appendix A, #3)

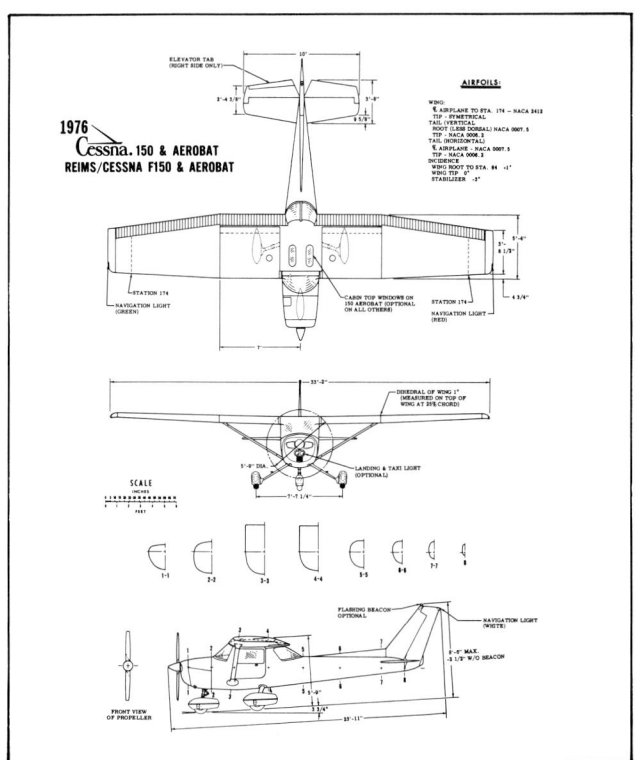

MODEL 150L/M ATC 3A19 1971-77

From 1971 to 1977 Cessna continued to refine the Model 150 until reaching the zenith of evolution in the 1977 150M version. Many changes had taken place, including new, tubular spring steel landing gear, longer dorsal fuselage fairing, landing light relocated to the engine cowling, a 3 inch forward extension of the propeller to reduce cabin noise and a completely new engine cowling originally introduced on the 1971 150L. The 1977 150M also benefitted from new wheel fairings found on the 1974 150L and the increased vertical stabilizer/rudder area of the 1975 150M. Only very minor interior changes and slightly redesigned wheel fairings occurred on the 1976 150M, including optional vertically adjustable seats, airspeed indicator readout in knots and circuit breakers to replace conventional fuses. 1977 signalled the end of Model 150 production after 22,769 Standard, Trainer, Commuter models and 1070 Aerobat versions had been produced. Total built: Domestic: 1977: 900; 1976: 1500; 1975: 1224; 1974: 931; Reims A150L/M: 1977: 90; 1976: 90; 1975: 105; 1974: 130; Price: approximately $17,000. Engine: Continental O-200A, 100 hp (150L/M, Rolls-Royce 0-240A, 130 hp, F150L/M series); gross weight: 1600 pounds; maximum speed: 125 mph; wingspan: 32 feet 2 inches; service ceiling: 14,000 feet. (Reference Appendix A, #4)

1977 Model 150M instrument panel.

1980 Model 152 II instrument panel with ARC RT-385A digital VHF transceiver.

MODEL 152   ATC 3A19   1978-80

Cessna made the transition from Model 150 to Model 152 in 1978 by introducing the Avco Lycoming O-235-L2C, four-cylinder opposed engine of 110 hp that was designed to burn 100 octane fuel. Other major changes were 28 volt DC electrical system, new McCauley propeller, engine oil cooler and flaps limited to 30 degrees extension (most Model 150s featured 40 degrees). Impulse couplings (designed to help start the engine) were on the left magneto only in 1978. One major servicing drawback of the 1978 model was the one-piece lower cowl that required propeller removal to take the cowl off. The 1979 Model 152 solved this problem with a split-nose cowling, had improved brake master cylinders and dual impulse couplings while the 1980 152 sported a new starter and carburetor accelerator pump to improve starting. Cessna included a spin-on type oil filter and more durable battery relay in 1981 and an avionics cooling fan was standard. Total built: Domestic: 1978: 2,265; 1979: 1,559; 1980: 949. Reims F152: 1978: 99; 1979: 144; 1980: 134. Model 152 first flight: 7-16-76; pilot: W.K. Bergman. (Reference Appendix A, #5)

MODEL A152   ATC 3A19   1981-84

The Aerobat series inherited the Lycoming engine in 1978 and continued its tradition as an aerobatic trainer. 1983 models featured the improved Lycoming O-235-N2C engine of 108 hp. Total built: Domestic: 1978: 74; 1979: 70; 1980: 65; 1981: 40; 1982: 28; 1983: 10; 1984: 2; 1985: 21; 1986: no c/n assigned. Reims Aviation FA152 airplanes used Lycoming O-235-L2C/O-235-N2C (1978/83 and after). Total built: Reims FA152: 1978: 11; 1979: 10; 1980: 15; 1981: 4; 1982: 4. Price: 1984: $36,750. Engine: Lycoming O-235-L2C, 110 hp (1978-82), O-235-N2C, 108 hp (1983); gross weight: 1670 pounds; maximum speed: 108 knots; wingspan: 33 feet two inches; service ceiling: 14,700 feet. (Reference Appendix A, #6)

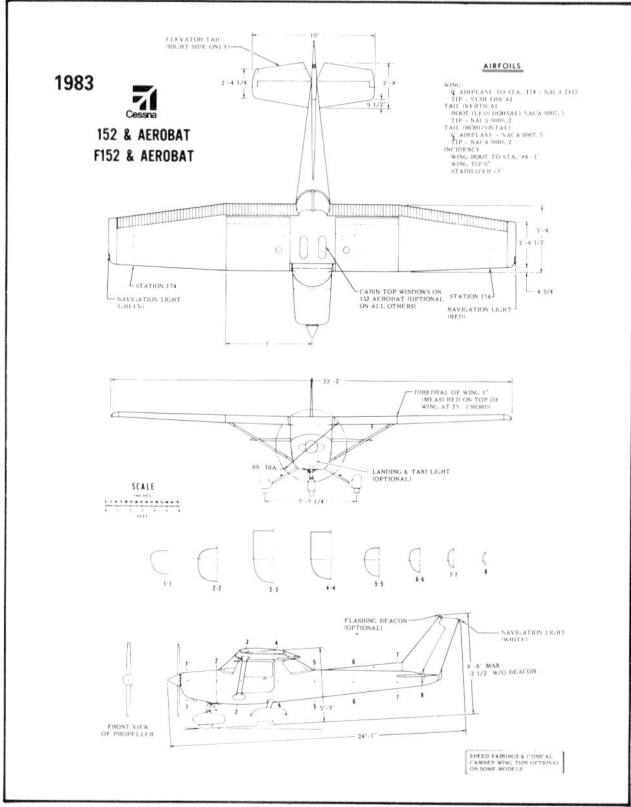

MODEL 152   ATC 3A19   1986

The only significant change for the 1986 Model 152 was the exterior paint scheme. Total built: Domestic: 1981: 620; 1982: 433; Reims F152: 1981: 84; 1982: 34; 1983: 14; 1984: 8; 1985: 12; 1986: no c/n assigned. Engine: Lycoming O-235-L2C, 110 hp (1982), O-235-N2C, 108 hp (1983); gross weight: 1670 pounds; maximum speed: 108 knots; wingspan: 33 feet two inches (Commuter); service ceiling: 14,700 feet. (Reference Appendix A, #7)

▲ MODEL 160 EXPERIMENTAL 1962
Designed as an inexpensive four-place airplane, only Model 160 (c/n 643) was built. Flight tests in 1962/63 showed promising performance but the project was abandoned and the airplane was stored until 1974 when it was scrapped. Fuselage and wing skin featured heavy beading for strength while reducing overall weight. Free-caster nose gear was employed for simplicity. Cessna proposed a Model 160M military version to the U.S. Army in 1964 as a low-cost FAC (Forward Air Controller)/utility airplane without success. Total built: 1962: 1 (c/n 643). Target price: proposed at $8450 (Model 160M proposed at $9850). Engine: Franklin 4A-225, 125 hp (Continental O-300-C, 145 hp intended for production airplanes), Continental IO-360, 210 hp intended for Model 160M; gross weight: 2050 (2450 - 160M); maximum speed: 134 mph (Franklin engine), 143 mph (Continental O-300-C), 173 mph (160M); wingspan: 34 feet seven inches; service ceiling: 14,200 feet (160), 18,200 feet (160M). Note: range: (26 gallons) 384 sm, 720 sm (160M); rate of climb: 660 fpm (1235 fpm - 160M).

▲ MODEL 170 PROTOTYPES   ATC 799   1947
Completely new from propeller to rudder, Cessna's Model 170 went from inception to first prototype in 9 months, with c/n 18000, NX41691 (illustrated) completed 11-5-47. Two more prototypes were built, c/n 18001 (NX41692) in December, 1947 and c/n 18002 (NX41693) in April, 1948. Metal fuselage/empennage with fabric-covered wing, the 170 was a comfortable four-place ship that hit the post-war market in 1948. Dual lift struts with jury braces were found on Model 170 airplanes only. Short-chord plain flaps were mechanically operated by floor-mounted lever in the cockpit and extended to 30 degrees. Aft cabin baggage compartment held 100 pounds and included small shelf for light items. Total built: 730. Price: 12-1-48: $5475. Engine: Continental C-145-2, 145 hp; Note: Cessna considered using the Jacobs O-360A, six-cylinder engine of 165 hp in June, 1946, but chose Continental's C-145; gross weight: 2200 pounds; maximum speed: 140 mph; wingspan: 36 feet; service ceiling: 15,500 feet.

▼   MODEL 170A   ATC 799   1949
The 1949 Model 170A was given a graceful, tapered all-metal wing with 64 inch chord out to the new, single lift strut and 43 inch chord to the wingtip. Other features of the wing were increased aileron and flap area, increased flap extension to 50 degrees and interchangeable wingtips (left/right). The flaps incorporated an up lock to prevent tailwinds from deflecting them when the ship was tied down. Wing landing lights were offered as an option for the first time (wiring was standard) and a Safe Flight stall warning horn was standard equipment. Total built: 470. Price: 1-1-49: $5995 (Edo Model 89-2000 floats and Federal A2500/A2500A skis were an option and could be factory or dealer installed). Engine: Continental C-145-2, 145 hp; gross weight: 2200 pounds (float version 2106 pounds); maximum speed: 140 mph (float version 115 mph); wingspan: 36 feet; service ceiling: 15,500 feet (float version 13,300 feet).

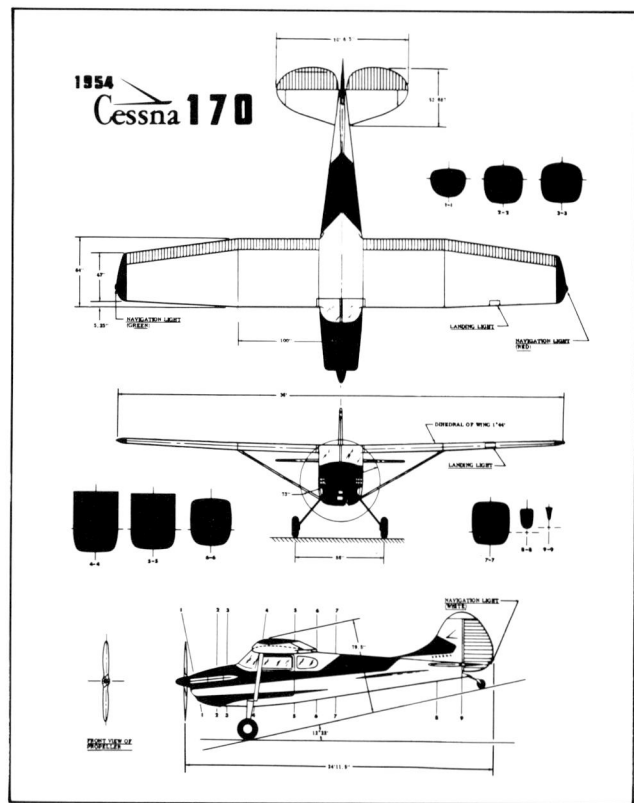

1950 Model 170A instrument panel. ▼

▲   MODEL 170A   ATC 799   1950-51

The 1950-51 Model 170A continued to sell in large numbers and propelled the classy four-place monoplane to new heights of popularity with private and business pilots. Short-chord plain flaps were retained but the 1951 170A was the last production version to use them. Improvements found on the 1950 170A included new cabin door seals and window latches, entry and exit straps on both doorposts, pilot seat raised to improve visibility, new interior fabrics and exterior paint scheme changed, redesigned engine cowling, fuel tank baffles at inboard section were installed to reduce sloshing. Crosswind landing gear was optional and an Aeromatic variable-pitch propeller was certified in 1951 and became optional during the 1951 production year (required Continental C-145-2H engine with drilled crankshaft). Major improvement on the standard C-145-2 was installation of dynamic dampers on the crankshaft that reduced engine vibration and cabin noise to more acceptable levels. Total built: 1066. Price: $6495. Engine: Continental C-145-2, 145 hp; gross weight: 2200 pounds (float version 2106 pounds); maximum speed: 140 mph (float version 115 mph); wingspan: 36 feet; service ceiling: 15,500 feet (float version 13,300 feet). Note: Edo Model 89-2000 floats and Federal A2500/A2500A skis optional at extra cost.

▼   MODEL 170B   ATC 799   1952-55

The Model 170B featured "High-Lift Flaps" (developed from the Korean War Cessna L-19 "Birddog") that extended back and down to 40 degrees, permitting slower landing speeds than the plain flaps used on the 170/170A. Empty weight increased 20 pounds to 1205 pounds (float version 1330 pounds), cabin soundproofing was improved, aft seat headroom was increased and baggage capacity was 120 pounds. Cessna called the Model 170B the "Businessliner", emphasizing the company's growing efforts to sell airplanes to increasing numbers of businessmen/pilots. N1625D, c/n 20267 (170B prototype) is illustrated at Wichita's municipal airport near the Cessna factory. Note optional landing light and wheel fairings. 1954/55 170Bs had redesigned, shock-mounted instrument panel, "Para-Lift" flaps. 1955 Model 170B had larger aft cabin windows, new tailwheel steering, new control wheels and cabin sun visors. Total built: 1952: 1108 (largest production run of 170 series); 1953: 666; 1954: 476; 1955: 491. Price: January 1, 1952: $7245; 1953: $8450; 1954/55: $8295. Engine: 1952-53; Continental C-145-2 (until c/n 25546, then C-145-2H was standard); 1955: C-145-2H engine designation became O-300-A, 145 hp; gross weight: 2200 pounds (float version 2106 pounds); maximum speed: 140 mph (float version 115 mph); wingspan: 36 feet; service ceiling: 15,500 feet (float version 13,300 feet).

▲   MODEL 170B   ATC 799   1956

1956 was the last production year for the highly successful Model 170 series. Major change from earlier versions was a completely new engine cowling. Minor improvements included increased windshield area (1200 square inches), improved defroster, revised instrument panel, lightweight, redesigned control wheels that permitted more legroom and a footrest for the right front seat passenger was included as standard equipment. Four exterior colors were offered: Scandia Blue, Burma Gold, Strato Blue and Cardinal Red. Empty weight increased to 1245 pounds. Illustrated is c/n 26963, N3420D, actually a 1955 c/n in 1956 paint scheme, employed as a 1956 model for marketing brochures. Total built: 175. Price: $8295. 5173 Model 170/A/B series airplanes (including all prototypes) were built over a nine year span. No 170Bs were built from January to October, 1956; five were built in November, 1956 and the last eleven airplanes were built in January, 1957 (there was no 1957 Model 170B placed in production). Cessna's one Model 170C was built (c/n 609, N37892) with 155 hp O-300-A engine and new empennage in November, 1954 but was later reconverted to a 170B and sold in January, 1956. The 170C series was not produced. (Reference Appendix A, #8)

▼   MODEL 170A FIELD MODIFICATION   1953

Art Whitaker of Portland, Oregon designed a simple but effective spray system for the Cessna Model 170 consisting of two wing-mounted supply tanks holding 86 total gallons of liquid. Air-driven pumps fed fluid to spray booms. The CAA approved Whitaker's installation under Part 08 and 03 permitting passengers to be carried after removal of the fans and dispersal brushes only. Tandem landing gear shown on 1950 Model 170A demonstrator was not part of the spray modification; normal landing gear was satisfactory.

▲ MODEL 172　　ATC 3A12　　1956

Cessna put a tri-cycle landing gear and new empennage design on the successful Model 170B airframe creating the ubiquitous and enormously popular Model 172 in 1956. Retaining the 170B's roomy four-place cabin and 145 hp O-300-A engine, the 172 series superceded the 170B on the production line. Shown above is c/n 612, N41768 that was originally a Model 170 (c/n 27053, N4499B), then a Model 170B prototype and finally served as the 172 prototype. Para-Lift flaps, Land-O-Matic main gear and steerable nose wheel were hallmarks of the first 172. Four exterior colors and a choice of red or blue interior were very similar to the 1956 170B. Total built: 1178. Price: 1956: $8750. Engine: Continental O-300-A, 145 hp; gross weight: 2200 pounds; maximum speed: 135 mph; wingspan: 36 feet; service ceiling: 14,300 feet.

Instrument panel for 1958 Model 172. ▼

▼ MODEL 172　　ATC 3A12　　1957-59

Few changes occurred on the 1957-59 Model 172, reflected primarily in exterior paint scheme design and minor interior refinements. The 1959 version featured a new cowling to improve engine cooling as illustrated on N8516B with optional wheel fairings. Most famous early 172 was N9172B that was flown by two pilots to an endurance record of 64 days, 22 hours, 19 minutes from December, 1958 to February, 1959. Total built: 1957: 1041; 1958: 750; 1959: 788. Price: 1957: $8975; 1958: $8995; 1959: $9250. Engine: Continental O-300-A, 145 hp; gross weight: 2200 pounds; maximum speed: 135 mph; wingspan: 36 feet; service ceiling: 13,300 feet.

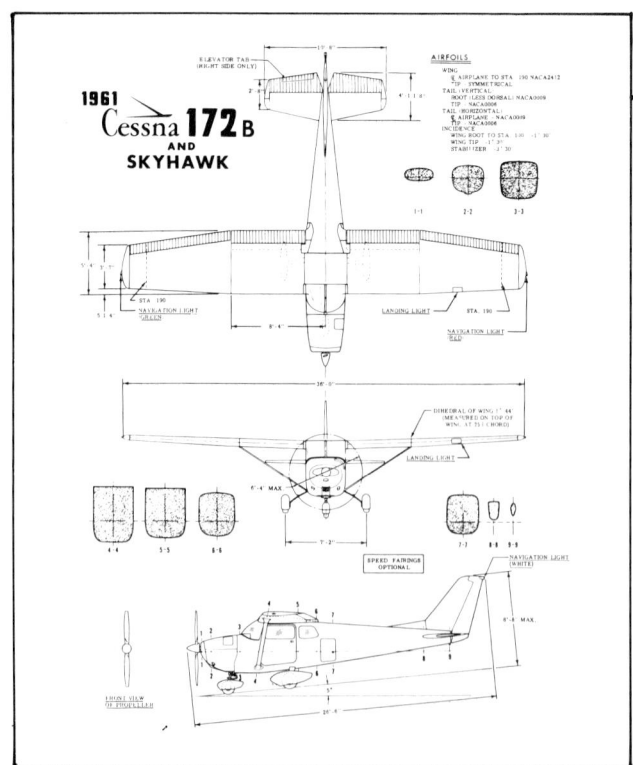

▲ MODEL 172A/B/C ATC 3A12 1960-62
The 1960 172A featured swept, "Flight-Sweep" tail as the first major change to the 172 series, and the 172A was the first version to be certified for floats. In 1961 the "Skyhawk" made its debut as the deluxe version of the Model 172, with special exterior paint and interior appointments, wheel fairings and more panel room for instrumentation. Main landing gear height was decreased three inches on the 1961 172B/Skyhawk to ease cabin entry/exit, engine mounts were lengthened three inches and surrounded by a new cowling topped off with a pointed propeller spinner. A baggage door was provided on the Skyhawk only. For 1962, the 172C received fiberglass wingtips and redesigned wheel fairings along with an increase in empty weight from 1325 to 1330 pounds. Illustrated is a 1960 172A, N34261 in standard exterior paint. Total built: 1960 172A: 994; 1961 172B: 989; 1962 172C: 810. Price: 1960 172A: $9450; 1961 172B Skyhawk: $11,475. Engine: Continental O-300-C, 145 hp (Model 172A/B/C), O-300-D (1961/62 Skyhawk); gross weight: 2200 pounds (1960/61), 2250 pounds (1962); maximum speed: 140 mph; wingspan: 36 feet (172A/B), 36 feet two inches (172C); service ceiling: 15,100 feet (172A/B), 14,550 feet (172C).

▼ MODEL 172D ATC 3A12 1963
1963 heralded another major change for the 172 series when the "Omni-Vision" aft fuselage/cabin window was made standard on 172D/Skyhawk. Other important changes were one-piece windshield, larger, redesigned rear cabin window, horizontal stabilizer/elevator span increased eight inches, folding hat shelf in rear cabin. Reims Aviation in France also built the 1963 F172D/Skyhawk. Photograph illustrates a 1963 Skyhawk that was Cessna's 50,000th (N50000) airplane built since 1934...a truly historical milestone. Total built: Domestic: 1011, Reims: 18. Price: $10,245 (172D), $11,995 (Skyhawk). Engine: Continental 145 hp O-300C (172D), O-300-D (Skyhawk); gross weight: 2300 pounds; maximum speed: 139 mph; wingspan: 36 feet two inches; service ceiling: 13,100 feet. (Reference Appendix A, #9)

▲ MODEL P172D ATC 3A17 1963
Basically a 172D with 175 hp engine and cowling of the Model 175, Cessna's 1963 P172D also featured the Omni-Vision rear window and eight inch increase to the horizontal stabilizer/elevator span but utilized a constant-speed propeller in place of the 172D's fixed-pitch unit. Known as the "172 Powermatic" and "Skyhawk Powermatic", the P172D possessed good performance and cabin comfort but was not very popular since it was marketed between the slower 172 and the faster Model 182. Reims also built the Powermatic as the FP172D. Total built: Domestic: 65; Reims: 3. Price: $13,275 (P172D), $14,650 (Skyhawk Powermatic). Engine: Continental GO-300-E (geared), 175 hp at 2400 rpm; gross weight: 2500 pounds; maximum speed: 146 mph (P172D), 148 (Skyhawk Powermatic); wingspan: 36 feet two inches; service ceiling: 17,000 feet. (Reference Appendix A, #10)

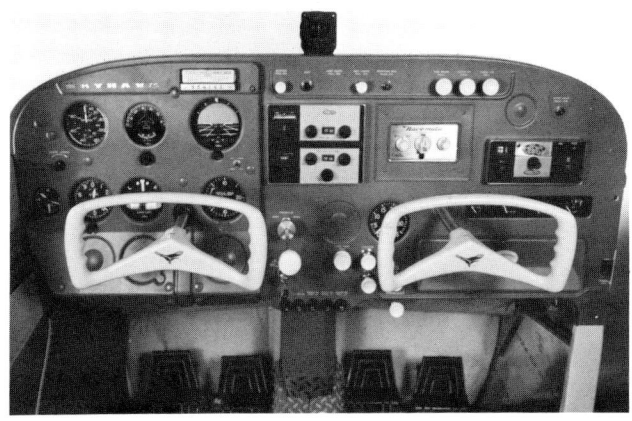

1963 Skyhawk instrument panel features Nav-O-Matic wing ▲ leveler, VHF transceiver and ADF avionics.

▼ MODEL 172E/F/G/H/I ATC 3A12 1964-68
Cessna changed to the 150 hp Lycoming O-320-E2D "Blue Streak" engine with the 1968 172I requiring cowling modifications, oil filler door and exhaust stack relocation

to the cowling top and right, lower cowl side respectively. The 172I featured all of the improvements found on the 172E (1964) through 172H (1967), such as redesigned instrument panel to accomodate center-mounted avionics and improved control knobs (172E), electrically-operated flaps and better instrument lighting (172F), new, longer propeller spinner and matching interior/exterior colors (172G), new wheel fairings, change to rotating beacon from flashing beacon, use of a 60 ampere alternator instead of generator, 11-point shock-mounted cowling and a 3-inch shorter nose gear oleo stroke (172H). Illustrated is N8293L (c/n 17256494) originally built as a late-year 172H painted in 1968 scheme. Total built: 1968 172I: 649; 1967 172H: 1586 (including 34 T-41A); 1966: 172G: 1474 (including 26 T-41A); 1965 172F: 1400 (including 170 T-41A); 1964 172E: 1209; Price: 1968: $11,700 (172I) and $13,250 (Skyhawk); Engine: Continental O-300-C, 145 hp (172E/F/G/H), O-300-D (Skyhawk); Lycoming O-320-E2D, 150 hp (172I/Skyhawk); gross weight: 2300 pounds (all models); maximum speed: 139 mph (172I: 140 mph); wingspan: 36 feet two inches (all models); service ceiling: 13,100 feet (all models). (Reference Appendix A, #11)

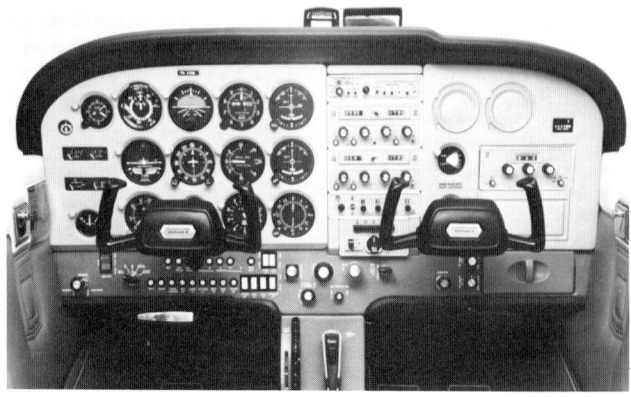
1976 Model 172M instrument panel.

▼ MODEL 172K/L/M   ATC 3A12   1969-76
Shown is N100M, a 1975 Skyhawk II, Cessna's 100,000th airplane. A summary of changes includes: 1969 172K: 5_08 increase in aft cabin window area, stabilizer/rudder tips recontoured, ground adjustable rudder trim tab; 1970 172K: conical camber wingtips; 1971 172L: cabin skylights optional, tubular steel landing gear, bonded baggage door, landing light in engine cowl; 1972 172L: dorsal fairing extended to Omni-Vision window, propeller diameter reduced one inch to 75 inches, bonded cabin doors, easier-to-operate instrument panel controls; 1973 172M: recambered leading edge on wing, rocker switches for lighting, key-locked baggage door; 1974 172M: "Skyhawk II" preferred options package available, 50% more baggage space, dual cowl-mounted landing lights, six mph increase in cruise speed; 1975 172M: inertia reel shoulder harness, improved instrument panel readout, better door seals; 1976 172M: increased cabin soundproofing, more avionics capacity in panel, vertical stabilizer recontoured. Total built: 1976 172M: 1900; 1973-75 172M: 4926; 1971-72 172L: 1535; 1969-70 172K: 2055; Price: 1969 Skyhawk: $13,995; 1976 Skyhawk: $20,750. Engine: Lycoming O-320-E2D, 150 hp; gross weight: 2300 pounds; maximum speed: 140 mph; wingspan: (1969 172K): 36 feet two inches; (1970 172K): 35 feet 10 inches; service ceiling: 13,100 feet (all models). (Reference Appendix A, #12)

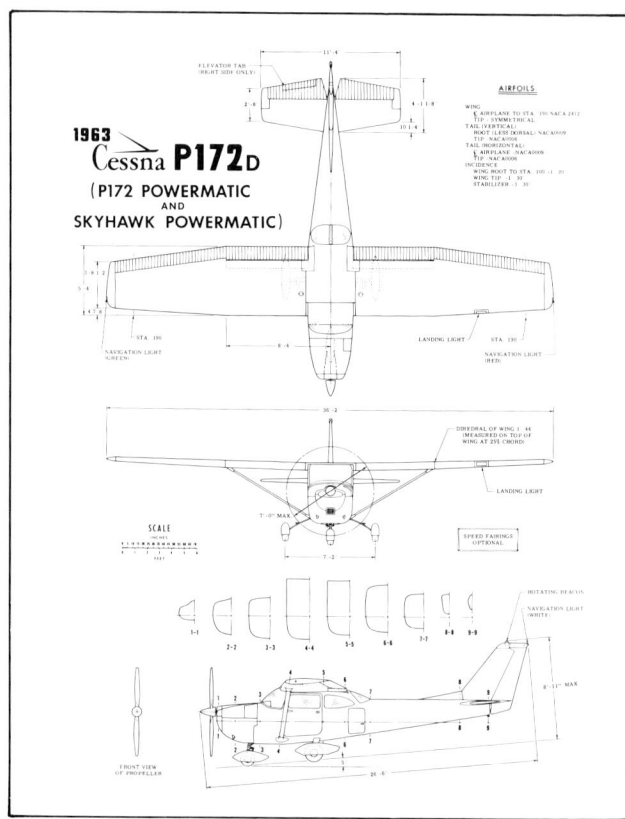

▼ MODEL 172N/P   ATC 3A12   1977-86
Cessna changed to the 160 hp Lycoming O-320-H2AD engine on the 1977 172N, designating it "Skyhawk/100" to reflect the 100 octane powerplant. In 1981 the O-320-D2J became the standard engine. Air conditioning was optional by 1981, pre-select flap control was standard on the 1977 Skyhawk; additional avionics capacity, low-vacuum warning light, thicker windshield/side windows and a second door latch pin were features of the 1984

Skyhawk. Cessna also offered "Nav-Pac" avionics options for IFR operations. As of 1985, Cessna had sold over 35,000 172/T-41/Skyhawk airplanes. Total built: 1985: 256; 1984: 179; 1983: 319; 1982 172P: 724; 1981 172P: 1025; 1980 172N: 1125; 1979 172N: 1850; 1978: 1725; 1977: 1725. Price: $49,600 (1985). Engine: Lycoming O-320-H2AD (1977-80), O-320-D2J (1981 and after); gross weight: 2300 pounds (172N), 2400 pounds (172P); maximum speed: 144 mph (172N), 123 knots (1984 172P); wingspan: 35 feet 10 inches; service ceiling: 14,200 feet (172N), 13,000 feet (1984 172P).

▲ MODEL 172Q   ATC 3A12   1983-84

Filling the gap between the Skyhawk and the 172RG, the 172Q Cutlass was introduced in 1983 with 180 hp engine, fixed-pitch propeller, 1,078 pound useful load and the ability to carry four 170-pound adults plus carry-on baggage. Standard features were: 3-cylinder priming for easy starting, dual controls, electric fuel boost/standby pump, fuel pressure gauge, gyro flight instruments with suction gauge, shoulder harnesses for all seats and an external baggage door. Air conditioning, 300 Series IFR avionics/Automatic Radial Centering optional. The 172Q was also offered as Cutlass II or Cutlass II/Nav-Pac. The Cutlass series was not produced in 1985/86. Total built: 1983: 210; 1984: 179. Price: 1984: $56,750 (Cutlass). Engine: Lycoming O-360-A4N, 180 hp; gross weight: 2550 pounds; maximum speed: 124 knots; wingspan: 36 feet one inch; service ceiling: 17,000 feet.

1981 Model 172P Skyhawk II instrument panel. ▼

▼ MODEL R172K   ATC 3A17   1977-81

Cessna introduced the R172K "Hawk XP" (extra performance) in June 1976. The experimental department built

1980 Cutlass RG II instrument panel.

1980 Model R172K Hawk XP II instrument panel. Note larger control wheels and horns.

a prototype (c/n 680) in 1973. A direct outgrowth of the FR172/T-41D series, the new XP was very similar to a standard Skyhawk except for the 195 hp fuel injected engine that was derated from 210 hp. A McCauley two-blade, constant-speed propeller was standard, a new cowling with integral landing lights, upgraded interior appointments and special exterior paint set the XP apart from its Skyhawk cousins. It was also available as the Hawk XP II version with preferred options package including full IFR avionics and heated pitot tube. It is interesting to note that the Hawk XP debuted one year (1977) before the Model 177/Cardinal entered its final year of production (1978) and was not offered after the 1981 model year. Neither the Cardinal nor Hawk XP could outsell or outlive the ubiquitous Skyhawk...Cessna's 'bread and butter' flying machine. All 1456 Hawk XP built (excluding c/n 680 built at Wichita) from 1977 to 1981 were produced at Cessna's Strother Field facility. Illustrated is N758UC, a 1981 model Hawk XP II demonstrator. Total built: 1977: 725; 1978: 205; 1979: 270; 1980: 200; 1981: 55. Reims Aviation built the Reims/Cessna Hawk XP (FR172K): 1977: 30. Price: 1977: $29,950 (Hawk XP). Engine: Lycoming IO-360-K (1977-79), IO-360-KB (1979-81) 195 hp; gross weight: 2550 pounds; maximum speed: 134 knots; wingspan: 35 feet 10 inches; service ceiling: 17,000 feet. (Reference Appendix A, #13)

MODEL 172RG   ATC 3A12   1980-1985

In 1980, Cessna exchanged the 172/Skyhawk's fixed gear for an electro-hydraulically operated retractable system, quickly making the new Cutlass RG a popular alternative to the higher-priced Model 182/182RG. A 2000-hour TBO (time between overhaul) 180 hp Lycoming engine and two-blade, constant-speed propeller, the Cutlass RG cruises at 140 knots at 75% power while burning only 10 gph (gallons per hour). Tubular steel main landing gear, pre-select flap control, gear unsafe light, fully carpeted baggage and reclining seats were standard equipment on the 1985 Cutlass RG with fully-articulating front seats, leather upholstery and a complete installation of IFR avionics optional. Over 1,100 Cutlass RG had been retailed to buyers by 12-31-84. Total built: 1980: 570; 1981: 320; 1982: 179; 1983: 44; 1984: 32; 1985: 13. Price: 1984: $73,900 (Cutlass RG). Engine: Lycoming O-360-F1A6, 180 hp; gross weight: 2650 pounds; maximum speed: 145 knots; wingspan: 35 feet 10 inches; service ceiling: 16,800 feet.

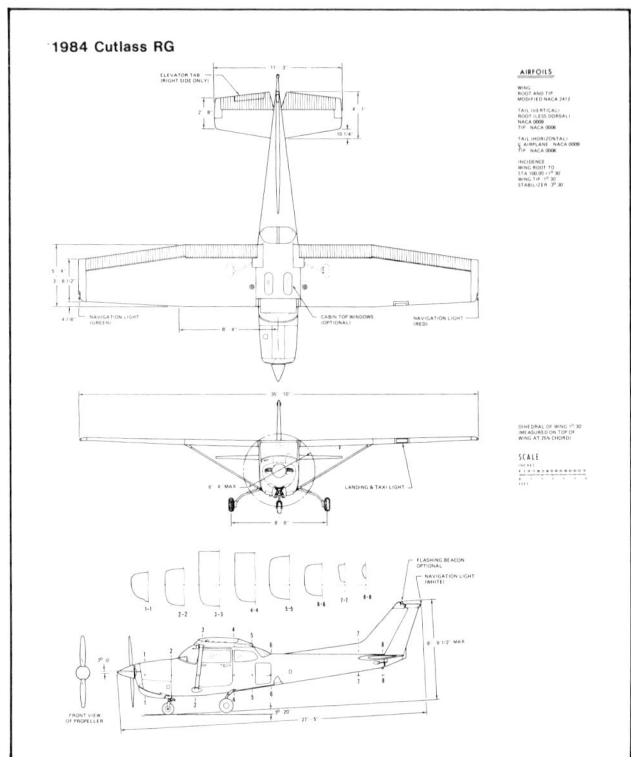

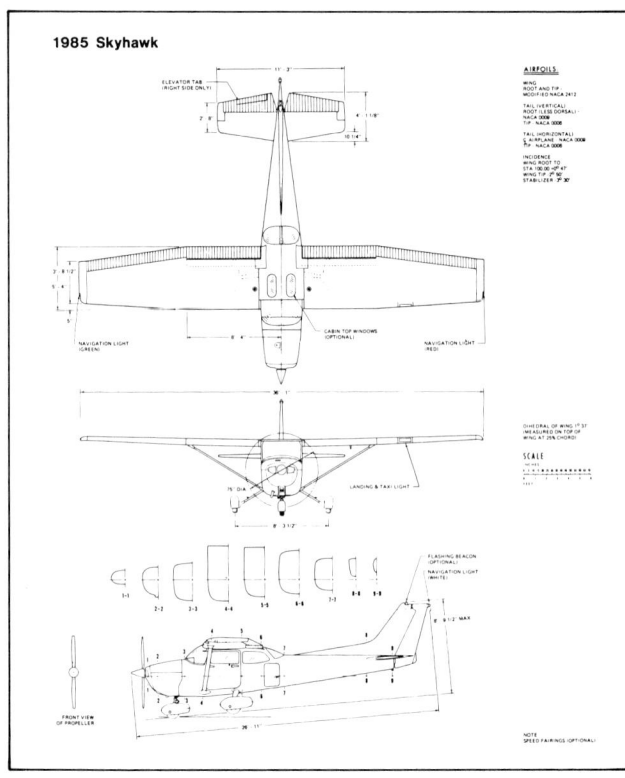

▲ T-41A ATC 3A12 1965-68

The U.S. Air Force purchased stock Model 172Fs for pilot training, designating them T-41A. The first batch of 170 airplanes were delivered in 1965 and leased by flight schools under contract to the air force. Both military serial number and U.S. registration number were displayed on the aircraft, as illustrated on first T-41A, N5100F, USAF s/n 65-5100, Cessna c/n 17251947. In 1966 Peru received 172G/T-41A through the Military Assistance Program. T-41A c/n were scattered throughout Model 172 F/G/H/K series c/n blocks. Total built: 1965 (172F): 170; 1966 (172G: 26; 1967 (172H): 34; 1970 (172K): 7. Price: negotiated. Engine: Continental O-300-D, 145 hp; gross weight: 2300 pounds; maximum speed: 139 mph; wingspan: 36 feet two inches; service ceiling: 13,100 feet. Note: only the two front seats were installed in T-41A aircraft. (Reference Appendix A, #14)

▼ T-41B ATC 3A17 1967

Officially named "Mescalero", the U.S. Army purchased modified R172E airplanes for primary/advanced pilot training as well as utility/transport work in support of army bases. Procured in 1967, the T-41B differed from the USAF T-41A version in having 210 hp, fuel-injected engine with two-blade, constant-speed propeller, 28-volt electrical system, openable right front cabin window, jettisonable doors, 6.00 x 6 nosewheel tire, no baggage door, fuselage/lift strut assist steps/cowl handle for fueling, Nav/Comm 300 VHF transceiver, AN/ARN 83 radio/antenna, provision for ARC 54 radio/antenna. Color was olive drab and white with flat black anti-glare panel on upper cowling, DayGlo lower cowl, wing/stabilizer tips. 25 T-41Bs were returned to Cessna in 1972 and rebuilt, with flat olive drab overall paint and returned to the army for possible MAP distribution. Army s/n 67-15000, Cessna c/n R172-0001 (illustrated) was first T-41B. Total built: 255. Price: negotiated. Engine: Continental IO-360-D, 210 hp; gross weight: 2500 pounds; maximum speed: 153 mph; wingspan: 36 feet two inches; service ceiling: 17,500 feet. (Reference Appendix A, #15)

▲ T-41C ATC 3A17 1968-83
In 1968 the USAF purchased T-41C aircraft for primary pilot training with 210 hp, fuel injected IO-360-D engine and fixed-pitch propeller. Airframe and cowling were same as army T-41B, but with 14 volt electrical system and standard Model R172E features. Finish was Alclad aluminum with flat black anti-glare panels. Both USAF serial number and U.S. registration number were applied to the airplanes. Total built: 1968: 45; 1969: 7. Price: negotiated. Engine: Continental IO-360-D, 210 hp; gross weight: 2500 pounds; maximum speed: 153 mph; wingspan: 36 feet two inches; service ceiling: 17,500 feet. Note: T-41C had only two fronts seats installed. (Reference Appendix A, #16)

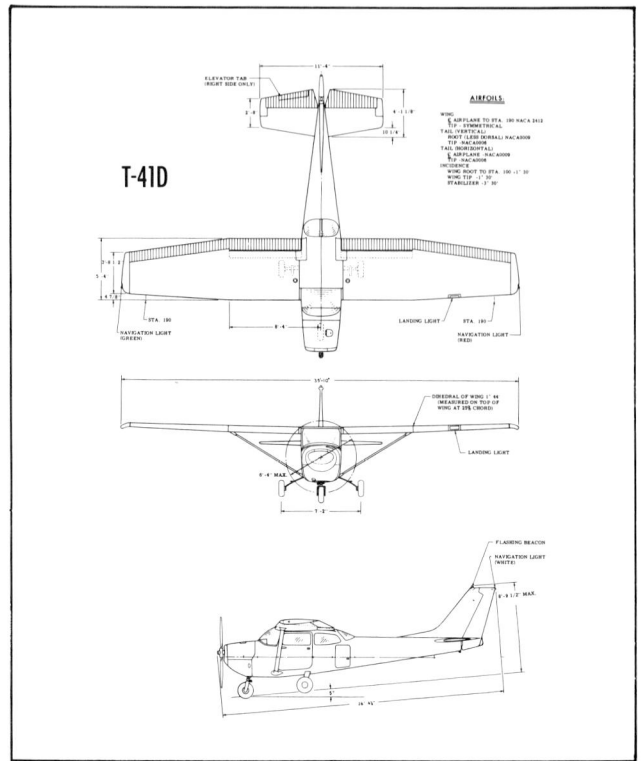

▼ T-41D ATC 3A17 1968-75
The T-41D had numerous features not found the T-41A/B/C, such as corrosion-proofing of stressed skin panels, four seats, reinforced flaps/ailerons, bonded cabin/baggage doors, horizontal stabilizer abrasion boots, provision for mounting wing pylons. T-41D purchased in 1972 (R172H) featured the long dorsal fairing of the Model 172L but did not incorporate the tubular steel main landing gear of the Model 172L, retaining the spring steel design. Reims Aviation had been building the 210 hp FR172 series since 1968 as the "Reims Rocket" and produced 60 in 1968 (FR172E), 85 in 1969 (FR172F), 80 in 1970 (FR172G), 125 in 1971/72 (FR172H), 240 in 1973/76 (FR172J). T-41D were similar to FR172E-H. Total built: 299 up to 1-1-75. 34 were R172E, 74 were R172F, 28 were R172G and 163 were R172H. Price: negotiated. Engine: Continental IO-360-D, 210 hp; gross weight: 2500 pounds; maximum speed: 153 mph; wingspan (with conical camber tips): 35 feet 10 inches; service ceiling: 17,500 feet. (Reference Appendix A, #17)

▲ MODEL 175   ATC 3A17   1958-59

In 1956, Cessna engineers took a Model 172, installed a geared engine and created the Model 175 series. Using a standard 172 (c/n 28700A) as the developmental testbed, the 175 was a four-place airplane that fit between the 172 and the popular but more expensive Model 182. First flight was on April 23, 1956. Changes from the Model 172 were a shock-mounted cowling and one-piece "Sight-Sweep" windshield. Adjustable front seats, electric fuel/oil gauges, safety-designed control wheels, panel-mounted fuel drain control, stainless steel mufflers were included as standard equipment. Wheel fairings were optional. Floats could be installed in the field. The 1959 175 was virtually identical to the 1958 version except for seven exterior color schemes (only four in 1958) were available, all applied over Alclad-treated aluminum and revised, more comfortable control wheels were made standard. N9205B (c/n 55005), an early production 1958 175 is illustrated. Model 175 was first production Cessna to utilize a geared engine. Total built: 1958: 702; 1959: 536. Price: $10,995. Engine: Six-cylinder Continental GO-300-A, 175 hp; gross weight: 2350 pounds; maximum speed: 147 mph; wingspan: 36 feet; service ceiling: 15,900 feet. Model 175 first flight: 4-15-57; pilot: R.W. Stephens.

MODEL 175A/B   ATC 3A17   1960-61 ▶

Major changes for the 1960 Model 175 were swept Flight-Sweep tail that added 18 inches to overall length (26 feet six inches). A deluxe version called the Skylark made its debut in 1960, with a higher empty weight of 1420 pounds compared to the 175A's 1339 pounds. An overall exterior paint scheme was standard on the Skylark only, along with wheel fairings and refined interior appointments. An external baggage door was standard on all 175A and the nose gear oleo travel was reduced three inches to improve ground handling characteristics. For the 1961 175B, an electric starter, new "Blend-Temp" heat/ventilation system was standard, reclining pilot/co-pilot seats were optional on either version. but only the Skylark offered an engine-driven vacuum system for gyroscopic flight instruments. Individual reclining front seats were optional but "Polycloud" posture padding was standard on the Model 175B and Skylark for 1961. Eight two-color exterior schemes (Model 175B) and eight three-color schemes (Skylark only) were available. 175A/B/Skylark were approved for float operations. Illustrated in this view is Skylark N3426D (c/n 619), 1960 175A production prototype. Total built: 1960: 540; 1961: 225. Engine: Continental GO-300-A, 175 hp; gross weight: 2350 pounds; maximum speed: 149 (Skylark); wingspan: 36 feet; service ceiling: 15,900 feet.

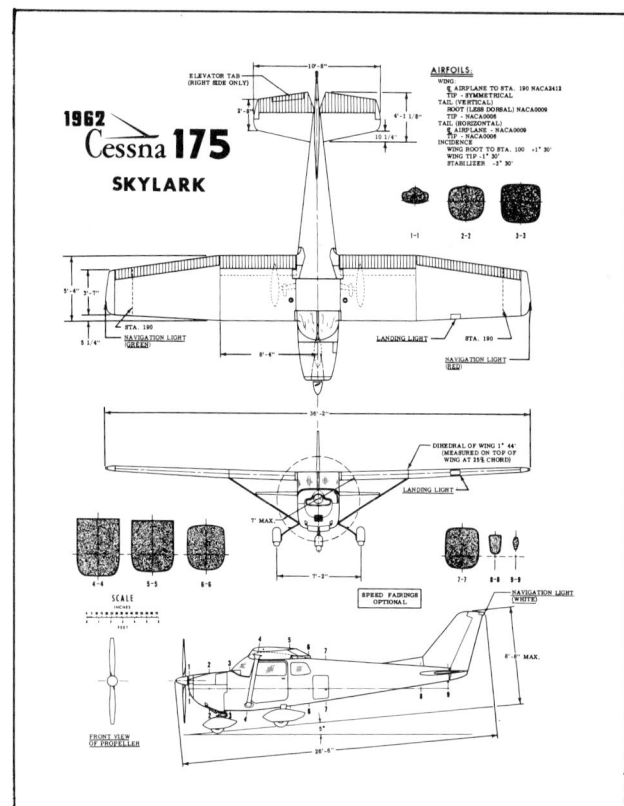

1959 Model 175 instrument panel.

▼ MODEL 175C ATC 3A17 1962

1962 was the final year of production for the Model 175 series after steadily decreasing sales from 1959 to 1961. Only the Skylark version was offered, with new wingtip fairings incorporating the position lights that increased wingspan two inches; revised cowling design, 100-pound gross weight increase, dual beam landing/taxi light in left wing leading edge and two-blade, constant-speed propeller with more pointed spinner were standard. Cowl flaps and cylinder head temperature gauge were new features of the 1962 175C/Skylark. All Model 175s and Skylarks (1958-62) had 52 gallon fuel tanks. The Skylark was FAA-approved for glider towing in 1962. First 1962 production Skylark, N8303T (c/n 17557003) is illustrated. Note the two-segment windshield, redesigned wheel fairings. Total built: 117. Price: $14,125. Engine: Continental GO-300-A, 175 hp; gross weight: 2450 pounds; maximum speed: 150 mph; wingspan: 36 feet two inches; service ceiling: 17,800 feet. Note: the Model P172 "Skyhawk Powermatic" was introduced in 1963, incorporating Model 175 engine and cowling. P172D replaced the Model 175 series.

▲ MODEL 177/CARDINAL   ATC A13CE   1968

Designed by a team of Cessna's engineers under the leadership of Ted Moody, the Model 177 (originally called the Model 341) featured a lightweight version of the Model 210's full cantilever, laminar flow wing with integral fuel tanks (wet cells) and a new fuselage design that positioned the pilot ahead of the wing leading edge. A stabilator was utilized to handle the forward c.g. created by the aft-mounted wing and tapered tubular steel main landing gear struts were selected for better shock absorption. A new instrument panel and flat cabin floor for increased passenger comfort completed the interior design of Cessna's airplane for the '70s. Prototypes N3765C (c/n 660) and N3766C (c/n 661) were used to obtain certification, with the first flight (c/n 660) on July 15, 1966. The basic Model 177 was introduced in late 1967 for the 1968 model year. The more expensive, deluxe Cardinal version was also offered in 1968 that included many interior/avionics options as standard equipment. The NACA 6400 airfoil selected for the Model 177 gave good cruise performance but higher stall speeds than the more docile 172. Cessna had intended the Model 177 to replace the venerable Model 172/Skyhawk, tagging the new design "Model 172J" (Skyhawk) but changed to 177 in late 1967, just prior to official model introduction to the public (no "J" Model 172 produced by Cessna). Flaps extended to 30 degrees using standard preselect control, fuel capacity was 49 gallons useable. Optional tanks not offered. Illustrated is the second prototype 177 with 1968 production year exterior finish. Total built: 1968: 1164 (production reached 12 per day for a short time in 1968). Price: $12,995 (Model 177); $14,500 (Cardinal). Engine: Lycoming O-320-E2D "Blue Streak", 150 hp; gross weight: 2350 pounds; maximum speed: 144 mph (Cardinal); wingspan: 35 feet 7 1/2 inches; service ceiling: 12,700 feet. Model 177 first flight: 7-15-66; pilot: William Robinson.

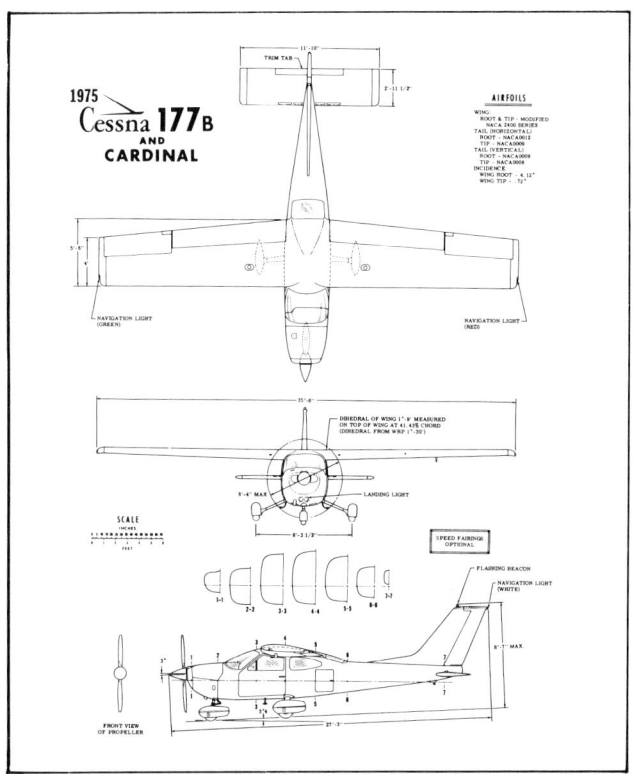

1969 Cardinal instrument panel featured down-curved ▼ glareshield and separate, integral chart compartment.

▼ MODEL 177A/B   ATC A13CE   1969-72

The 1969 Model 177A featured 180 hp, smaller tail fairing for better ground clearance, 100% balanced, slotted stabilator that improved control response at slow speeds.

Increased gross weight and redesigned interior were incorporated to improve the 177's performance and sales appeal. Later models featured many changes; summarized by year: 1970: constant-speed propeller, new cowl/cowl flaps, redesigned stabilator mount, Camber-Lift wing (NACA 2400) for better slow airspeed handling; manifold pressure/cylinder head temperature gauges; 1971: cowl-mounted landing light, instrument panel/sub-panel padding, bonded baggage door; 1972: key-locked baggage door, bonded upper cowl, seat belt/shoulder harness for both front seat occupants were standard. Total built: 1969: 206; 1970: 160; 1971: 103; 1972: 140. Price: (1970): $17,500 (Cardinal). Engine: Lycoming O-360-A2F, 180 hp (1969); O-360-A1F6, 180 hp (1970-72); gross weight: 2500 pounds; maximum speed: 153 mph (Cardinal); wingspan: 35 feet six inches; service ceiling: 14,600 feet. N1902F (c/n 1770002) illustrated was 177B prototype.

1977 Cardinal II instrument panel. ▲

177B   ATC A13CE   1973-75 ▶

Changes for the 1973 Model 177/Cardinal were: maximum speed increase (3 mph) from aerodynamic cleanup, more streamlined cowl, new optional 60 gallon (useable) fuel tanks, improved cabin door sealing; 1974: new interior styling and thicker, contoured seat cushions for better comfort, subpanel rocker switches; 1975: introduction of Cardinal II with preferred options package, cruise speed increase of seven mph from landing gear/brake fairing redesign, improved engine baffles/lower cowl airflow, new propeller and a tachometer green arc up to 2700 rpm allowing 75% power at 10,000 feet. Total built: 1973: 200; 1974: 150; 1975: 190. Price: $24,980 (1975 Cardinal II). Engine: Lycoming O-360-A1F6D, 180 hp; gross weight: 2500 pounds; maximum speed: 160 mph (1975 Cardinal II); wingspan: 35 feet six inches; service ceiling: 14,600 feet. 1975 Cardinal II illustrated.

▼   MODEL 177B   ATC A13CE   1976-78

Cessna continued to improve the 177/Cardinal in 1976 with a totally redesigned instrument panel permitting more room for avionics and locating engine instruments in front of the pilot while the 1977 model featured a revised interior including an energy-absorbing, collapsible lower sub-panel, vernier mixture control and seven cabin color choices. For 1978, Cessna offered the Cardinal Classic that was loaded with special standard equipment such as full IFR avionics/flight instruments, post lights, heated pitot tube, EGT gauge, special royal cherry wood laminate instrument panel, silver-color control wheels and unique "Cardinal Classic" exterior logo. Steadily decreasing sales, high prices, consistent popularity of the 172/Skyhawk and the 1977 introduction of the Hawk XP caused Cessna to terminate the Model 177/Cardinal after 1978. Total built: 1976: 209; 1977: 150; 1978: 80. Price: $35,350 (1977 Cardinal II). Engine: Lycoming O-360-A1F6D, 180 hp; gross weight: 2500 pounds; maximum speed: 160 mph (1977 Cardinal II); wingspan: 35 feet six inches; service ceiling: 14,600 feet.

▲ MODEL 177B EXPERIMENTAL 1971
Cessna installed a Curtiss-Wright (Wankel-type) engine in c/n 661, N3766C for "quiet airplane" research conducted by Curtiss-Wright and Cessna under a U.S. Navy program. Rated at 185 hp, the liquid-cooled powerplant required an extensive muffling system (note long exhaust stack under fuselage, exit at tail) and a 100-inch diameter, three-blade propeller for noise reduction. Tests indicated that decibel levels were significantly reduced with the rotary-type Wankel powerplant/muffling system. Model 1023 first flight: 7-7-71; pilot: L.R. Ikerd.

MODEL 177RG   ATC A20CE   1971-78   ▶
The fixed-gear 177 went retractable in 1971 with Cessna's introduction of the Cardinal RG (original designation Model 1008/Reims F1008, changed to 177RG/Reims F177RG) with a 1500 psi electro-hydraulic retraction system. Gross weight, horsepower and speed were increased with Cardinal RG series. A summary of changes by year includes: 1972: cabin steps retracted with gear, drag reduction and new propeller increased cruise speeds; 1973: recontoured cowl design, 60 gallons (useable) fuel capacity, improved cabin door seals, cowl-mounted taxi/landing lights, hydraulically-operated downlocks; 1974: gear control handle with direct linkage to powerpack system; 1975: Cardinal RG II with preferred options package, 1976: new, lightweight gear retraction system, redesigned instrument panel; aluminum nose gear trunnion, airspeed indicator primary scale in knots, 1977: instrument sub-panel redesigned, fuel selector standardized with other Cessna single-engine models; 1978: 28-volt electrical system, improved gear powerpack, avionics master power switch. 1978 was the last production year for Cardinal RG series. Total built: 1971: 161 (Reims 42); 1972: 70 (Reims 20); 1973: 150 (Reims 30); 1974: 160 (Reims 30); 1975: 195 (Reims 16); 1976: 264 (Reims 22); 1977: 214 (Reims 17); 1978: 100). Price: $51,395 (1978 Cardinal RG II). Engine: Lycoming IO-360-A1B6, 200 hp (1971/72); IO-360-A1B6D, 200 hp (1973); gross weight: 2800 pounds; maximum speed: 156 knots (1978); wingspan: 35 feet six inches; service ceiling: 17,100 feet. Illustrated is a 1978 Cardinal RG II. (Reference Appendix A, #18). Model 177RG first flight: 2-16-70; pilot: L.R. Ikerd.

1976 Cardinal RG instrument panel. ▲

▲   MODEL 180   ATC 5A6   1953

The Model 180 was Cessna's high performance four-place airplane in the early 1950s. N41697, c/n 604 (illustrated) was the prototype. A new empennage design marked the first production departure from the familiar rounded tail long used on Cessna airplanes. Para-Lift flaps, spring steel landing gear, constant-speed propeller, 225 hp six-cylinder engine, steerable tailwheel and all-metal construction were standard. First flight was January, 1952, with the first production airplane coming off the line in October and type certification granted in December. Total built: 641. Price: $12,950. Engine: Continental O-470-A, 225 hp; gross weight: 2250 pounds; maximum speed: 165 mph; wingspan: 36 feet; service ceiling: 19,800 feet. Model 180 first flight: pilot: Hank Waring.

▼   MODEL 180   ATC 5A6   1954-56

Changes to the 1954/55 180 were primarily interior refinements for improved passenger comfort. The 1956 model featured a 230 hp engine, new air intake duct and new exterior paint scheme as illustrated on N4599B, a 1956 Model 180. Wheel fairings were optional. Large, cockpit-controlled cowl flaps are shown in the closed position. Total built: 1954: 620; 1955: 891; 1956: 512. Price: $12,950. Engine: Continental O-470-A and J, 225 hp (1954); O-470-J, 225 hp (1955); O-470-K, 230 hp (1956); gross weight: 2550 pounds; maximum speed: 165 mph; wingspan: 36 feet; service ceiling: 19,800 feet.

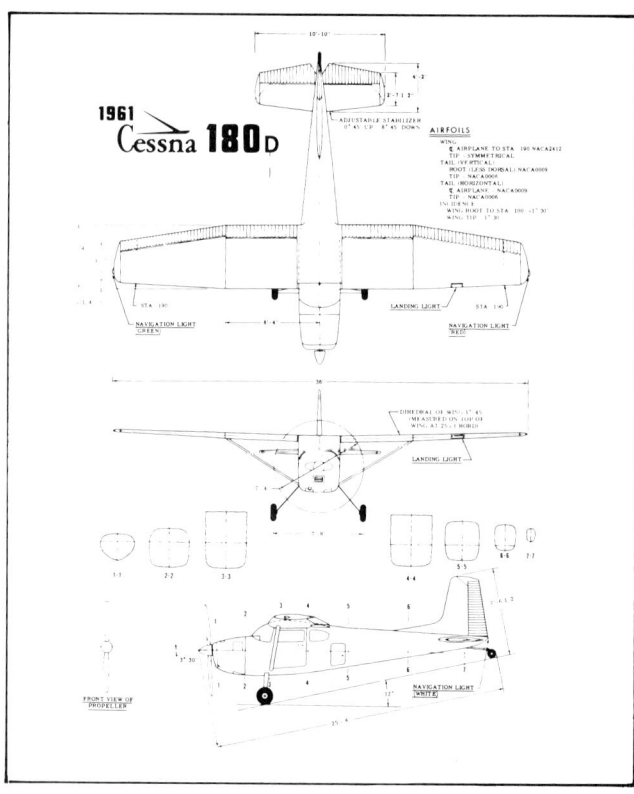

▼   MODEL 180A/180F   ATC 5A6   1957-63

The highly successful Model 180 received only minor changes from 1957 to 1963, including: 1957/58 180A: revised instrument panel and sub-panel switches, improved tailwheel steering, single-action parking brake; 1959 180B: completely redesigned instrument panel with relocated instruments and engine cluster gauges; 1960 180C: revised cowling with front-mounted air intake filter; 1961 180D: instrument panel redesigned for increased avionics capacity; 1962 180E: fuel tanks redesigned to incorporate two outlet ports, increased useable fuel and provision for optional (84 gallons) tanks (65 gallons standard), new wing tips and position light mounts; 1963 180F: semi-reclining front seats, instrument panel lighting controls in overhead panel, new rudder pedals and standardized Cessna instrument panel knobs. Eight 180E bought under Military Assistance Program as U-17C by U.S. Army in 1962. The first 1963 Model 180F, N2684Y (c/n 18051184) is illustrated. Total built: 1957: 444; 1958: 250; 1959: 306; 1960: 251; 1961: 152; 1962: 112 (including 8 U-17C for MAP); 1963: 129. Price: $15,950 (1963 180F). Engine: Continental O-470-K, 230 hp (1957-60); O-470-L, 230 hp (1961); O-470-R, 230 hp (1962); gross weight: 2650 pounds; maximum speed: 170 mph (180F); wingspan: 36 feet (180A/D), 36 feet two inches (180E and F); service ceiling: 21,500 feet.

▼ MODEL 180G/H   ATC 5A6   1964-72

The 1964 180G represented a big change for the 180 series when it inherited the Model 185's fuselage with third cabin window (except for firewall), 185 wings/landing gear and provision for a utility seat in the aft cabin giving it six-place capability. Dorsal fairing on the 180 was not as deep or long as the Model 185 and remained the primary visual difference between the 180 and 185. Both airframes were nearly identical by 1965 when Cessna installed the Model 185 firewall in the 180H. Improvements for the 180H included: 1965-67: redesigned instrument panel to accomodate center-mount avionics, improved fuel strainer, pointed propeller spinner (1967), improved door latches (1966), increased stowage area in aft cabin (1967), optional auxiliary door on left side available (1967), Aeroflash rotating beacon (1967); 1968-72: metal-to-metal seat belts and stowable rudder pedals (right side only); 1970-72: new wingtip design, exterior paint scheme remained virtually the same for three years, 300-pound external cargo pack available on 1970 180H. All 180s after 1964 featured alternators. Total built: 1964: 133; 1965: 162; 1966: 167 (3 U-17C); 1967: 101 (3 U-17C); 1968: 118; 1969: 110; 1970: 72 (3 U-17C); 1971: 46; 1972: 63. Price: $21,350 (1972 180H). Engine: Continental O-470-R, 230 hp; gross weight: 2800 pounds; maximum speed: 170 mph; wingspan: 36 feet two inches (1964-69), 35 feet 10 inches (1970); service ceiling: 19,600 feet. Illustrated is N5421E, c/n 645, 180G prototype (originally built as 180C).

1966 Model 180 instrument panel accomodated center-mounted avionics.

1968 Model 180 instrument panel featured open—view control wheels.

Cessna lineup for 1954: 170B, 180, 195, 310.

▲ MODEL 180J/K ATC 5A6 1973-81

1973 Model 180J featured new "Camber-Lift" wing with bonded leading edge, revised instrument panel/rocker switches, cowl-mounted landing/taxi lights; 1974 180J had optional cabin door bubble/observation windows for increased downward visibility. The 1975/76 180J was unchanged except for exterior paint scheme while the 1977 180K featured a vernier mixture control for its higher compression Continental engine, relocated heater plenum on firewall, strengthened tailwheel and flight instruments grouped in basic "T" configuration on instrument panel. 1977 also marked 25 years of continuous Model 180 production. The new "Skywagon II" with preferred options package debuted in 1978 and only minor changes occurred in the series until Cessna terminated production in favor of the Model 185. The last 180 c/n assigned was 18053203, N20642 and the last 180 built was c/n 18053202, completed 9-10-81 (both ships were Model 180K). A 1979 180 II is illustrated. Total built: 1973: 100; 1974: 116; 1975: 120; 1976: 150; 1977: 135; 1978: 95; 1979: 115; 1980: 52; 1981: 36. Price: $41,910 (1978 Skywagon II). Engine: Continental O-470-R, 230 hp (1973/74); O-470-S, 230 hp (1975/76); O-470-U, 230 hp (1977); gross weight: 2800 pounds; maximum speed: 170 mph; wingspan: 35 feet 10 inches; service ceiling: 19,600 feet (180J), 17,700 (180K).

▼ MODEL U-17C ATC 5A6 1962-1970

Cessna sold 18 Model 180s to the U.S. military for use by friendly foreign powers. Basically an "off the shelf" airplane except for olive drab exterior paint finish, 8 were built in 1962, 3 in 1966 and 1967 and 3 in 1970. Originally referred to as Model 180E or 180H, designations were later changed to U-17C for all 17 airplanes. U-17C illustrated is 16th ship, c/n 18052172 in olive drab overall with yellow numerals/markings, no national insignia. Specifications same as Model 180E or 180H. (Reference Appendix A, #19)

1976 Model 180J instrument panel. ▲

1980 Model 180 II instrument panel. ▲

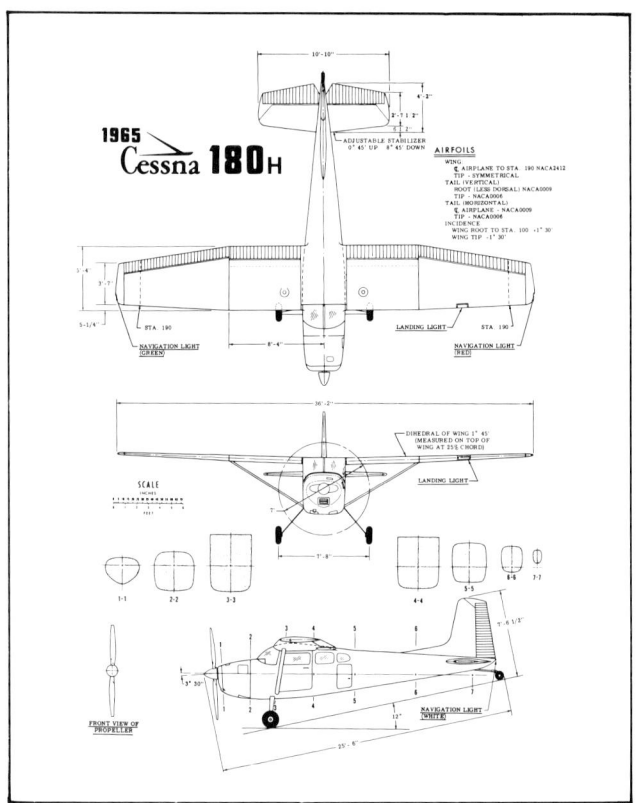

Top Performer... Now Proved and Improved

It's '54's "Smoothest" Airplane

America's most widely acclaimed new airplane—the powerful Cessna 180—now offers you greater performance, beauty and value than ever in a brilliant 1954 model! Completely service-proved —refined and improved in dozens of ways, it's quieter and smoother, cruises over 150 m.p.h., offers full 4-place comfort, brilliant new interior and exterior colors and styling and yet the Cessna 180 is still $6000 *under* the nearest competitor. Only $12,950!

Smoothest Power Possible

...So smooth that when the engine is running, you can even rest a glass of water on the cowling without disturbing the water! ...flashing 6-cylinder power with automobile economy. Eight brand-new engine improvements.

"Living Room" Comfort Aloft

Step in! Stretch out! Here you'll find more foot and leg room, more over-all comfort than in any other airplane in the 180 class. A powerful heating-ventilating system keeps you comfortable in every season, at every altitude.

No Other Airplane Can Match Cessna 180's All-Round Performance!

New Exterior Baggage Door... New Color Striping... New Upholstery... New Sloping Map Compartment..."Para-Lift" Flaps...World's Safest, Smoothest Landing Gear... Extra Sound-Proofing...Gravity-Feed Fuel System (60 gals.)... Easy conversion for skis, floats or cargo. For more information, see nearest Cessna dealer (listed in yellow pages of your telephone book) or write Cessna Aircraft Co., Dept. F-2, Wichita, Kansas.

FLYING—February 1954

▲ MODEL 182   ATC 3A13   1956

A spinoff of the rough and ready Model 180, the 1956 Model 182 featured tri-cycle landing gear and redesigned cowling as the major departures from the conventional gear 180. The first production 182 was completed on January 30, 1956 while N41782, c/n 613 (illustrated) performed prototype flight test duties. The four-place 182 promised to be a fast, efficient and popular ship for pilots who preferred tri-cycle landing gear. 1956 constructor numbers were: c/n 33000 through 33842. Total built: 844. Price: $13,750. Engine: Continental O-470-L, 230 hp; gross weight: 2550 pounds; maximum speed: 160 mph; wingspan: 36 feet; service ceiling: 19,000 feet. Model 182 first flight: 9-10-55; pilot: E.B. Feutz.

▼ MODEL 182A/B   ATC 3A13   1957-59

1957/58 Model 182 received significant changes, starting with the 182A of 1957 featuring main landing gear lowered four inches, increasing gear track 5.4 inches for better ground handling and beefing up main gear struts from 11/16 inch to 3/4 inches thick. Interior refinements included stronger seat frames, rear seats with better back support, upholstery rolled around door frames for more finished appearance, new, flush door latches, key-locked baggage door, redesigned instrument panel and fuel gauges; generator low voltage annunciator standard equipment. Flaps were manually operated and extended to 40 degrees. A deluxe 182 called the "Skylane" was introduced in 1958 with standard overall exterior paint scheme and wheel fairings, the exhaust stack was moved to the right side of the improved cowling that increased cylinder cooling airflow. 1959 changes included more streamlined cowling, cowl flaps were made standard equipment, improved rear seat ventilation, black Royalite instrument panel cover and second chart box. Illustrated is 1958 production Model 182 Skylane. Total built: 1957: 911; 1958: 802; 1959: 802. Price: $17,095 (1959 Skylane), $14,600 (182). Engine: Continental O-470-L, 230 hp; gross weight: 2650 pounds; maximum speed: 170 mph (Skylane); wingspan: 36 feet; service ceiling: 19,800 feet.

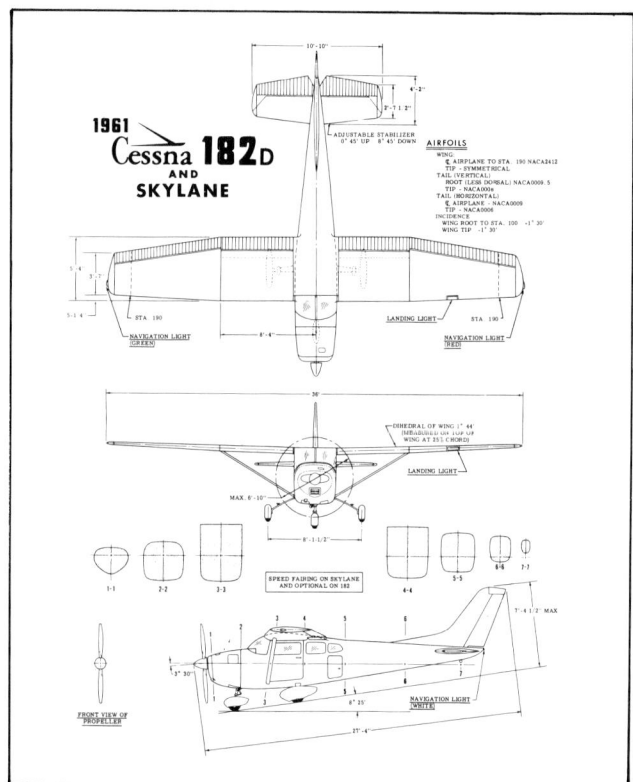

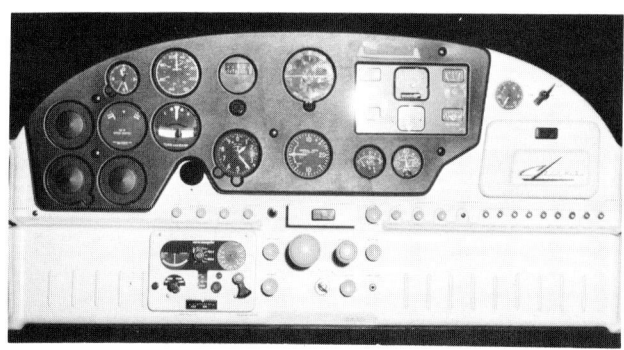

1957 Model 182 instrument panel (control wheel/shaft ▲ removed). Note square tachometer in engine cluster.

MODEL 182C/D   ATC 3A13   1960-61

Primary change for 1960 182C/Skylane was Cessna's swept tail that increased overall length 25 inches to 27 feet four inches. A third cabin window was added, flush-fitting fuel caps and increased cabin headroom, molded plastic control wheels, "Polycloud" seat cushions, smaller wing root fillets. In 1961 a key-operated start switch was standard, cam-lock fasteners on cowling for easy maintenance access, gear height decreased four inches for better passenger entry and exit. Total built: 1960: 650; 1961: 591. Price: $17,950 (Skylane). Engine: Continental O-470-L, 230 hp; gross weight: 2650 pounds; maximum speed: 170 mph (Skylane); wingspan: 36 feet; service ceiling: 19,800 feet. N2323G, c/n 51623 illustrated was 1960 prototype Skylane.

MODEL L-19L   ATC 3A13   1961

Cessna built four 1961 Model 182D as L-19L for the Canadian National Defense (CDN) Army. All four were virtually identical to commercial versions with 230 hp Continental O-470-L engine and equipped with wheel fairings. L-19L 16727, c/n 53153 illustrated. Specifications were same as Model 182D. Note open cowl flaps, ADF reception equipment, optional horizontal stabilizer abrasion boots, pilot seat extended headrest, anti-glare cowl panel and left wing landing light. Price: negotiated. (Reference Appendix A, #20)

MODEL 182E   ATC 3A13   1962

After building over 4,500 182/Skylanes since 1956, Cessna completely revamped their popular four-place design in 1962. Principal changes were: new fuselage with "OmniVision" rear windows, flat, 3/4 inch lower, four inch wider cabin floor that increased head, shoulder and leg room, new instrument panel/control pedestal with rocker-type switches, electrically-operated "Para-Lift" flaps (first 182 to have them), redesigned horizontal stabilizer and elevator/rudder trim tabs, seamless wingtips, new tailcone and wheel fairings, neoprene rubber fuel bladders holding 65 gallons total; dual gravity feed ports with 25% larger diameter; new, stronger main landing gear/fuselage attachment and improved nose wheel steering. Payload increased 140 pounds; empty weight increased by only 10. Shown above is N34266, c/n 634 that served as the 182E prototype. Total built: 826. Price: $18,490 (Model 182 Skylane). Engine: Continental O-470-R, 230 hp; gross weight: 2800 pounds; maximum speed: 170 mph (Skylane); wingspan: 36 feet two inches; service ceiling: 18,900 feet.

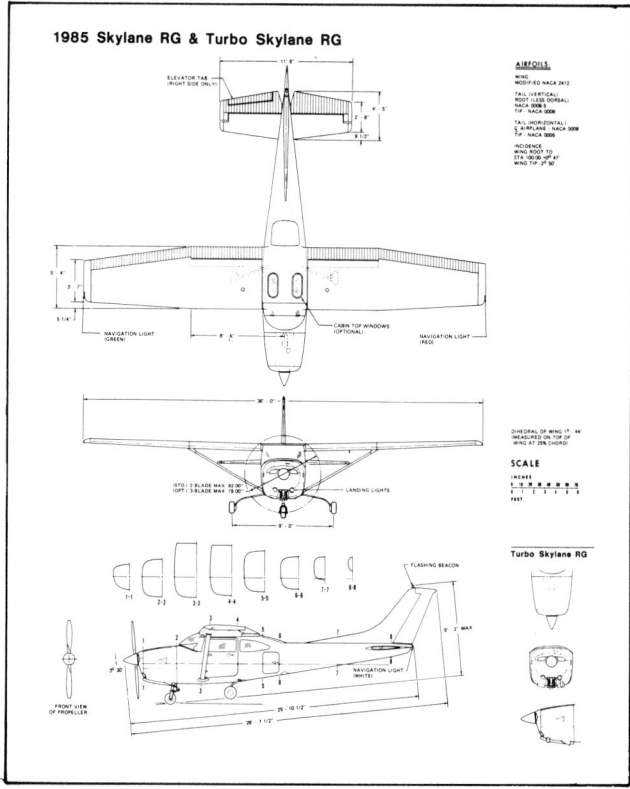

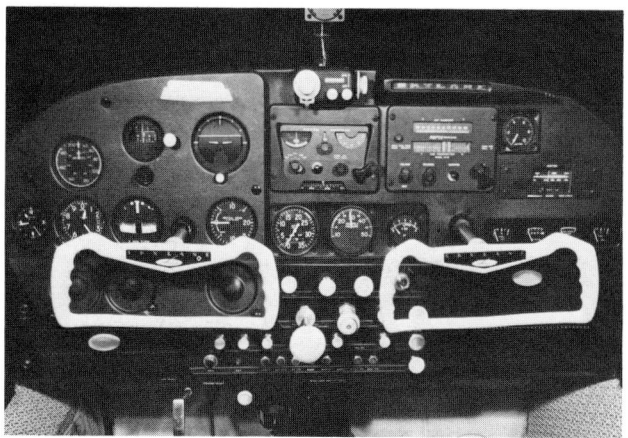

1959 Skylane instrument panel featured two chart compartments and black plastic Royalite cover.

▲ MODEL 182F/M   ATC 3A13   1963-69

The 1963 182F had few changes from the 182E, primarily magnesium rudder pedals, minor refinements to interior/exterior details. Major change for 1964 was a one-piece rear window and reshaped, longer aft cabin window for increased viewing area. 1965 182H: new propeller spinner increased length by one inch, horizontal stabilizer/elevator span increased 10 inches to 11 feet eight inches, thicker, one-piece windshield without center post; 1966 182J: magnesium control wheels, new cabin door latches 1967 182K: short stroke nose gear oleo, verticial stabilizer tip increased overall length by 2 1/2 inches, "Omni-Flash" rotating beacon; 1968 182L: new boom mike, pre-select flap control, flight instruments relocated in front of pilot; 1969 182M: turn coordinator standard on Skylane only. N6504F, a 1967 Skylane is illustrated. Total built: 1963: 635; 1964: 786; 1965: 840; 1966: 941 (less 56 shipped to Argentina as A182J); 1967: 880 (less 40 shipped to Argentina as A182K); 1968: 820 (less 20 shipped to Argentina as A182L); 1969: 750. Price: $19,950 (1969 Skylane). Engine: Continental O-470-R, 230 hp; gross weight: 2800 pounds; maximum speed: 170 mph (Skylane); wingspan: 36 feet two inches; service ceiling: 18,900 feet. (Reference Appendix A, #21)

▼ MODEL 182M EXPERIMENTAL   1967

In July, 1967 Cessna built the experimental 182M with a full cantilever wing using N3768C, c/n 662 (illustrated) as the testbed. The cantilever wing was part of a 1965 proposed Model 343 (Model 187) using a 240 hp Continental GIO-336 engine. The Model 187 project was cancelled but Cessna elected to flight test the wing on a stock Model 182. After only four hours of flight tests the project was dropped because of manufacturing costs of the wing coupled with negligible boost in performance. This is the first photograph of the Model 182M ever published. Cessna also flew an experimental Model 182 with a plastic Dow/Windecker wing on 10-15-65; pilot: W.M. Robinson.

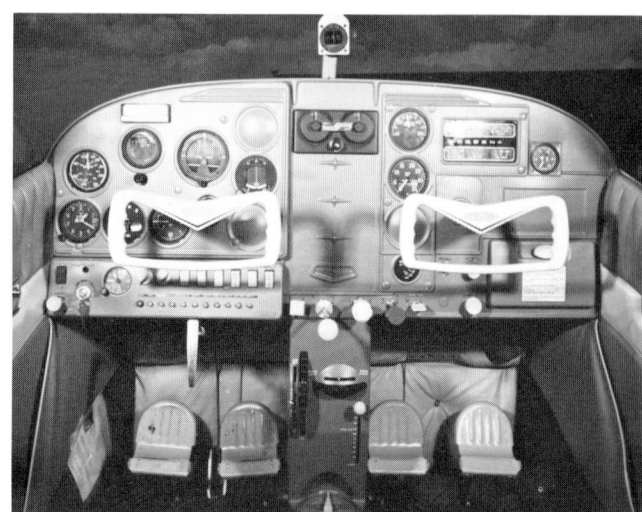

1962 Model 182E Skylane featured redesigned instrument ▲ panel and electric flap control for first time in a Model 182.

▼ MODEL 182N/Q   ATC 3A13   1970-77

Cessna continued to refine the 182 series with the following model year changes: 1970 182N: conical camber wingtips reduced overall wingspan by 4 inches, revised instrument panel, new, more streamlined cowl; 1971 182N: increased cabin soundproofing, standard shoulder harness for front seats only; 1972 182P: restyled cowling incorporating landing/taxi lights, new tubular steel main landing gear struts increased main gear track width 13 1/2 inches to 109 inches, "Camber-Lift" wing with bonded, recontoured leading edge, push-button annunciator panel, restyled control wheels (note: Argentine-built A182N incorporated all these improvements); 1973/74 182P: shock-mounted cowling, bonded cowl and cabin doors, extended dorsal fairing; 1974 182P: tighter cabin door/window seals, redesigned front doorposts, new engine cooling baffle seals and constant-speed propeller; 84 gallon fuel tanks and oxygen system optional; 1975/76 182P: new wheel/brake fairings; 1976 182P: improved wing root fairing reduced cabin noise level, O-470-S engine; 1977 182Q: O-470-U engine developing 230 hp at 2400 rpm (previously 2600 rpm), new instrument panel fasteners, vernier mixture control, padded sub-panel. 1975 Model 182P Skylane II is illustrated. Total built: 1970: 390; 1971: 380; 1972: 621 (less 20 Argentine-built A182N); 1973: 1040; 1974: 1010; 1975: 820; 1976: 880; 1977: 790 (Reims built 25 F182P in 1976 and 39 F182Q in 1977). Price: $34,950 (Skylane II). Engine: Continental O-470-R, 230 hp (1970-74), O-470-S, 230 hp (1975/77) O-470-U, 230 hp at 2400 rpm (1977); gross weight: 2950 pounds; maximum speed: 148 knots (Skylane); wingspan: 35 feet 10 inches: service ceiling: 17,700 feet (182N/P), 16,500 feet (1977 182Q).

MODEL 182R/T182R   ATC 3A13   1986
Significant change to the 182/Skylane series after 1977 was availability of turbocharging first offered on the 1981 T182 but deleted from the option list in 1986. No major improvements were made to the 182R series that began in 1981. Air conditioning was optional on the Model 182R but not available on the 1986 Skylane. Refinements to the interior and instrument panel on the 182R series included flat black panel color and redesigned glareshield, new choice of seat fabrics/colors. 1986 Skylane N9432X is illustrated. Total built: 1978: 624; 1979: 709; 1980: 414; 1981: 339; 1982: 237; 1983: 74; 1984: 65; 1985: 106. Price: $34,950 (1977 Skylane). Engine: Continental O-470-U, 230 hp; Lycoming 0-540-L3C5D, 235 hp (T182); gross weight: 3100 pounds; maximum speed: 146 knots; wingspan: 35 feet 10 inches; service ceiling: 14,900 feet.

MODEL R182/TR182   ATC 3A13   1978-86
The 182 went retractable in 1978, using a hydraulic retraction system similar in operation to Cardinal RG series. Officially known as the R182 but marketed as the Skylane RG, Cessna's newest four-place speedster had a useful load of 1,378 pounds and a rate of climb of 1140 fpm. A 235 hp Lycoming O-540-J3C5D, six cylinder engine sat under a new cowling that was 15 1/2 inches longer than the Continental-powered fixed-gear 182/Skylane. The 1979 R182 had 88 gallon fuel capacity (76 in 1978) and turbocharging was offered for the first time. No major changes occurred in the series between 1979 and 1986. Total built: 1978: 583; 1979: 729; 1980: 314; 1981: 169; 1982: 129; 1983: 44; 1984:25; 1985:31. Reims also built the FR182, producing 21 in 1978, 24 in 1979 and 24 in 1980 when FR182 production stopped. Price: $49,950 (1978 Skylane RG), $106,650 (1986 Skylane RG). Engine: Avco Lycoming O-540-J3C5D, 235 hp; O-540-L3C5D, 235 hp (Turbo Skylane RG); gross weight: 3100 pounds; maximum speed: 160 knots (Skylane RG), 187 knots (Turbo Skylane RG); wingspan: 35 feet 10 inches (1978), 36 feet (1985); service ceiling: 18,000 feet (Skylane RG), 20,000 feet (Turbo Skylane RG). Model R182 first flight: 8-27-76; pilot: T.E. Wallis

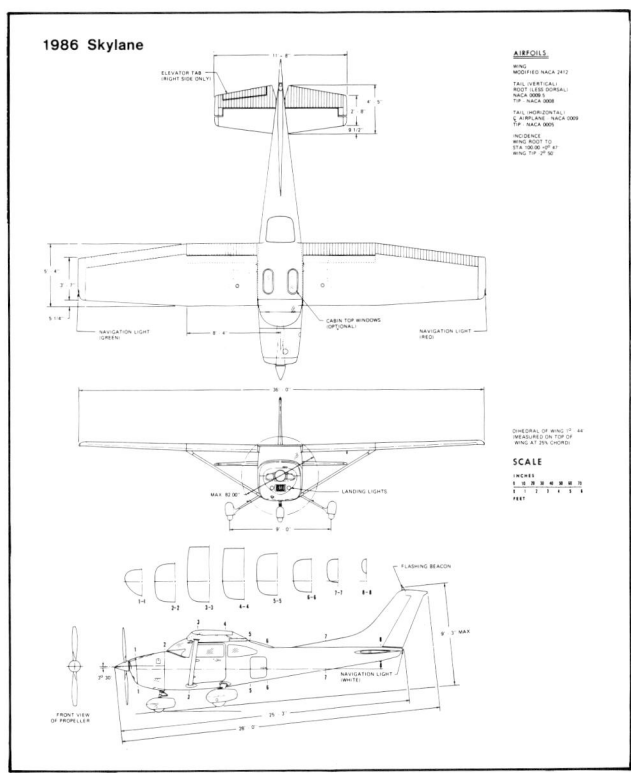

1976 Model 182P instrument panel.

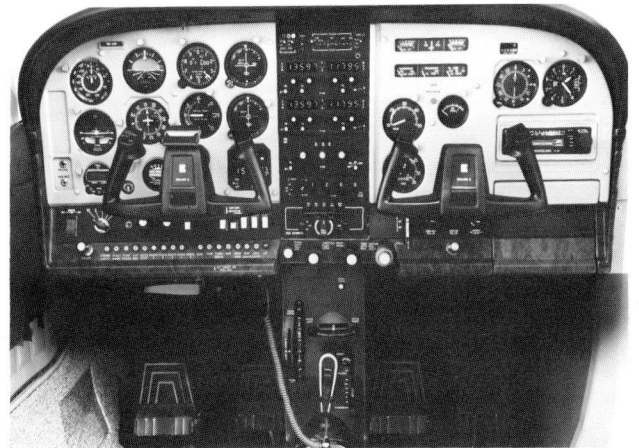

1980 Skylane II instrument panel with ARC digital nav/com avionics.

Now... Over 150-m.p.h. cruising speed plus the big new feature that makes flying like driving!

NEW CESSNA 182
with LAND-O-MATIC* landing gear
The patented feature that revolutionizes flying

You've read about it. You may have tried it in the new Cessna 172. And now you can get amazing new Land-O-Matic landing gear in a new high-speed Cessna... the great new Cessna 182.

This airplane has everything. <u>Unequalled ease of handling</u>—you drive it up; you drive it down; you can turn and park it easier than an automobile. <u>Cruising speed that measures up to airplanes costing thousands of dollars more.</u> "Hush-flight" quietness and new luxury that make long trips a pleasure. See it. Drive it. Only $13,750 f.o.b. Wichita. See your Cessna dealer (listed in Yellow Pages of phone book) or write CESSNA AIRCRAFT CO., Dept. F-10, Wichita, Kansas.

Inquire about Cessna lease plans

5 GREAT CESSNAS—THE COMPLETE AIR FLEET FOR EVERY BUSINESS NEED
- 170
- 172
- 180
- 182
- 310

Cessna®

"Picture window" visibility   Wide-span Land-O-Matic   20 sq. ft. of reserve lift

FLYING—September 1956

▲ MODEL 185   ATC 3A24   1961
To complement the rugged and reliable Model 180, Cessna introduced the nearly identical 185 in 1961. Primary visual change from 180 was a recontoured, deeper dorsal fairing that the 185 has retained throughout its production lifespan. With a useful load of 1620 pounds, the Model 185 quickly became a popular load-hauler. Built to work, the 185 had heavy-duty axles, tires and landing gear and an optional cargo-pak that could hold 300 pounds. 65 gallon fuel tanks were standard with 84 gallon tanks/two-speed electric fuel pump optional (mechanical pump standard). With room for six adults, the Model 185 was powered by a 260 hp, fuel-injected Continental engine swinging a two-blade, constant-speed propeller. Two extra cabin windows were also standard and the 185 was approved for floats and skis. 1962 Model 185 prototype was c/n 632, shown here as N34272 in 1961 finish. Total built: 238. Price: $18,950. Engine: Continental (six-cylinder) IO-470-F, 260 hp; gross weight: 3200 pounds (185's 1620-pound useful load was greater than its empty weight of 1520 pounds); maximum speed: 176 mph; wingspan: 36 feet; service ceiling: 17,300 feet.

▼ MODEL 185A/B/C/D/A185E   ATC 3A24 1962-69
Called the Skywagon in 1962, few major changes occurred to Model 185 series between 1962 and 1969. Yearly improvements were: 1962 185A: new wingtips with integral position light increased span two inches, vernier throttle/mixture controls, two electric auxiliary fuel pumps; 1963 185B: overhead light console, die-cast magnesium rudder pedals, one electric auxiliary fuel pump; 1964 185C: 52 ampere, 12-volt alternator, manual tailwheel lock, dual brake linings; 1965 185D: instrument panel featured center-mount avionics, open-view control wheels, integrated engine instrument cluster; 1966 185E/A185E: 100-pound gross weight increase on 185E, 285 hp engine optional as A185E with 150-pound gross weight increase, 1967 A185E: 285 hp engine standard, pointed propeller spinner increased overall length three inches, extended rear cabin compartment, "split-bus" electrical system, individual center passenger seats, 60 ampere alternator; 1968 A185E: gross weight increased 50 pounds, new, automatic induction air system, metal-to-metal seat belts, new baggage door, seat adjustment handles; 1969 A185E: new 300/400-series ARC avionics available. Total built: 1962: 275; 1963: 141 (including 63 U-17A); 1964: 124 (including 34 U-17A); 1965: 191 (including 83 U-17A); 1966: 183 (including 72 U-17A. Note: In 1966, 66 were 185E, 45 were

A185E); 1967/68/69: 450 (including 13 U-17A, 61 U-17B). Price: $22,450 (1969). Engine: Continental IO-470-F, 260 hp (1962-66), IO-520-D, 285 hp (1966); gross weight: 3200 pounds (1962-66), 3300 pounds (1966 A185E), 3350 pounds (1968); maximum speed: 178 mph; wingspan: 36 feet two inches; service ceiling: 17,150 feet (1969 A185E). (Reference Appendix A, #22)

▲ MODEL A185E/F/AGCARRYALL   ATC 3A24 1970-77
An optional side-loading door on the left fuselage side made loading bulky cargo easier and conical camber wingtips decreased wingspan four inches in the 1970 A185E. A new version called the "Agcarryall" was introduced in 1972 with external 151 gallon chemical tank, removeable spray booms with 30 nozzles, wind-driven spray system, windshield wire cutters and vertical stabilizer cable deflector. A 1973 AGcarryall, N70222 (c/n 18502066) is illustrated. Total A185E/F built (1970-72): 347 (including 144 U-17B) and eight 1972 AGcarryall. Price: $25,140 (A185E), $29,475 (AGcarryall). Engine: Continental IO-520-D, 285 hp continuous (300 hp takeoff); gross weight: 3350 pounds; maximum speed: 178 mph (A185E), 148 (AGcarryall); wingspan: 35 feet 10 inches; service ceiling: 17,150 feet (A185E), 13,400 feet (AGcarryall).

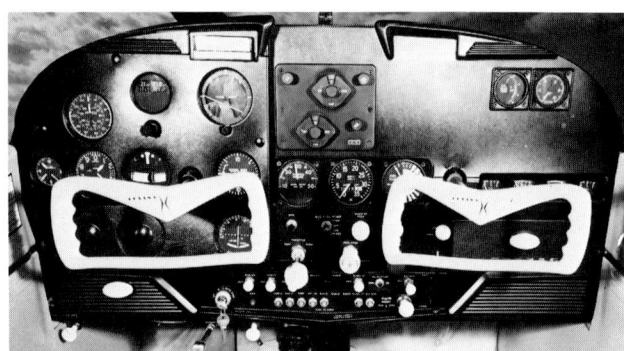

1962 Model 185 instrument panel. ▲

MODEL A185F/AGCARRYALL   ATC 3A24 1973-85
Cessna's "Camber-Lift" wing was installed on the Skywagon 185/AGcarryall in 1973 along with dual, cowl-mounted landing/taxi lights, split-rocker master switch, redesigned instrument panel with shadow gray escutcheon and padded control wheels. Bulged upper cabin door windows and flat lower cabin door windows were optional on 1974-75 A185F. 1976 A185F featured new polycarbonate heater outlets and optional "Honeycomb" nylon seating fabric for cold-weather climates, airspeed indicator primary scale in knots. 1977 Skywagon 185s had stronger tailwheel gear/spring, redesigned control wheels, improved fuel selector valve, Improvements for 1978-85 included: 28-volt electrical system, avionics master power switch, flush-mounted window latch and introduction of the 185 Skywagon II preferred options package with IFR avionics, while a three-bladed propeller, polyurethane paint became standard in 1980. An EGT was standard on the 185 Skywagon II and black instrument panel escutcheon was optional. Total built: 1973: 203 (including 7 AGcarryall); 1974: 240 (including 15 AGcarryall); 1975: 242 (including 31 AGcarryall); 1976: 297 (including 18 AGcarryall); 1977: 304 (including 16 AGcarryall); 1978: 225 (including 7 AGcarryall); 1979: 255; 1980: 200; 1981: 185; 1982: 70; 1983: A185F: 20; 1984: 8; 1985: 23; 1986: no c/n assigned. As of 1982, 3916 185s had been built since 1961. Price: $41,750 (1978 185 Skywagon); $48,700 (185 Skywagon II). Engine: Continental IO-520-D, 285 hp (300 hp takeoff); gross weight: 3350 pounds; maximum speed: 155 knots; wingspan: 35 feet 10 inches; service ceiling: 17,150 feet. 1980 185 Skywagon illustrated with optional wheel fairings.

▼ MODEL U-17A   ATC 3A24   1963
Cessna built a military version of the Model 185 equipped with standard commercial features. These airplanes were delivered to friendly foreign governments for armed forces work. Illustrated is U-17A s/n 63-13024, a 1963 Model 185B assigned to the 112th Liason Squadron of the VNAF, based at Tan Son Nhut Air Base, South Vietnam (photograph taken 12-14-70). Note non-standard size right center cabin window, modified flat black anti-glare panel contours, VNAF insignia. Total built (all U-17A): 1963 185B: 63; 1964 185C: 34; 1965 185D: 83; 1966 185E: 72; 1967 185E: 13. Price: negotiated. Engine: Continental IO-470-F, 260 hp; gross weight: 3200 pounds (185B/C/D), 3300 pounds (185E); maximum speed: 172 mph (185E); wingspan: 36 feet two inches; service ceiling: 16,600 (185E). (Norman E. Taylor photograph via Bob Pickett).

▲ MODEL U-17B   ATC 3A24   1967-73
American help through the Military Assistance Program (MAP) continued with the U-17B series, built from 1967 to 1973. Basically a standard Model A185E/F, batches of U-17B were ordered for six years. Total built (all U-17B): 1967: 26; 1968: 9; 1969: 26; 1970: 94; 1971: 12; 1972: 38 (1967-72 were A185E); 1973: 10 (A185F). Price: negotiated. Engine: Continental IO-520-D, 285 hp; gross weight: 3350 pounds; maximum speed: 178 mph; wingspan: 36 feet two inches (1967-69), 35 feet 10 inches (1969-73); service ceiling: 17,150 feet. U-17B, s/n 71-1457, a 1971 A185E, is illustrated. (Reference Appendix A, #23)

▼ MODEL 187 EXPERIMENTAL   1968
In the spring of 1968 Cessna engineers developed the Model 187, a new airplane intended to replace the four-place Model 182 series for the 1970s. A full cantilever wing similar in construction to the Model 210 and a T-tail with balanced stabilator was selected, with swept-forward, tubular steel main landing gear. The project started life in July, 1965 as the Model 343 with 240 hp Continental GIO-336 engine but was redesignated Model 187 in 1968 with a 240 hp Continental O-470 Spec 32 engine. Despite promising flight tests, the Model 187 offered no significant improvements over the 182/Skylane series and was cancelled. N7167C, c/n 666 (the only airplane built) is illustrated with conventional empennage but was also tested with a T-tail. Note intentional design similarity to the 177/Cardinal series. Engine: Continental O-470-R, 230 hp; gross weight: 2900 pounds; maximum speed: 167 mph (estimated); wingspan: 35 feet four inches; length: 27 feet 4 1/2 inches; height: seven feet 11 3/16 inches (T-tail); rate of climb: 900 fpm; range: 1000 statute miles (89 gallons). This is the first photograph published of the Model 187. Model 187 first flight: 4-22-68; pilot: W.H. Ohnsieder.

▲ MODEL 188 PROTOTYPE 1965
Cessna entered the agricultural aircraft market in 1965 with the Model 188 Agwagon. The prototype, c/n 651, N5424E, (illustrated) made its first flight on February 19, 1965. A completely new design, the Agwagon featured many safety and drag-reducing features not incorporated on all contemporary ag airplanes, including all-metal airframe construction with a tough, welded 4130 chrome molybdenum steel tube fuselage structure from the cockpit forward covered with aluminum panels; the aft fuselage was semi-monocoque stressed skin and the empennage was designed for heavy-duty operations; compression struts attached the outer wing panels to the fuselage and were the only external bracing on the aircraft; 360-degree pilot visibility, 7/8-inch thick, heavy-duty main landing gear struts, fuel tank located behind firewall; quick-egress cockpit doors, hopper tank was situated in front of cockpit and directly on the airplane's center of gravity (CG). Wings had six degrees of dihedral for ground clearance and increased stability in flight. Pre-production changes included a revised fuselage structure with the landing gear carry-through truss relocated to the front spar, compression struts mounted higher on the fuselage and pilot's seat relocated for better access to cockpit components. Total built: 2 (c/n 651/653). Engine: Continental O-470-R, 230 hp; gross weight: 3300 pounds; maximum speed: 130 mph; wingspan: 41 feet two inches; service ceiling: 10,000 feet. Model 188 first flight: 2-19-65; pilot: R.D. Reagan

▼ MODEL 188/A188 ATC A9CE 1966-67
Agwagon production began in March, 1966 with two models, the 188/Agwagon 230 with 230 hp/fixed-pitch propeller and the A188/Agwagon 300 with 300 hp and constant-speed propeller. All Agwagons had triple corrosion-proofing, epoxy primer/finish paint and stainless steel flight control cables were standard. A wire deflector cable from top of canopy to top of the vertical fin was standard; windshield/landing gear wire cutters optional. Manually-operated wing flaps (30 degrees maximum extension) were mounted outboard of the landing gear to minimize ground debris damage. An eight-inch tail wheel and 8.00 x 6 main gear tires, 14-volt electrical system were standard. Flight/spray control instruments were positioned on a small panel directly in front of the pilot at near eye level for quick scanning. A 200-pound capacity liquid/dry material hopper featured top loading with side-loading systems optional. The first production Model 188 Agwagon, c/n 188-0001, is illustrated. Total built: 188: 139; A188: 178. Price: $15,995 (188), $18,995 (A188). Engine; Continental O-470-R, 230 hp (188), IO-520-D, 285 hp continuous (A188); gross weight: 3300 pounds (normal category); 3800 pounds (188, restricted category), 4000 pounds (A188, restricted category); maximum speed: 119 mph (188), 151 mph (A188); wingspan: 40 feet 4 1/2 inches; service ceiling: 9600 feet (188), 10,400 feet (A188).

1966 Agwagon instrument panel was designed for minimum ▶ pilot workload.

▲ MODEL 188/A188A   ATC A9CE   1968-71

Three years of experience with the 188/A188 brought many changes to the Agwagon series by 1968 when Cessna introduced the Agwagon A with standard improvements including: stronger hopper walls, strengthened elevator/horizontal stabilizer spars, skin stiffeners, 28-volt electrical system with alternator for night operations, vented fuel tank encased in PVC plastic envelope to contain crash fuel spill. In 1970 the Agwagon B arrived with wing dihedral increased to 9 degrees, wing airflow fences/aileron gap seals for improved low-speed control, canopy top/rear windows standard, maximum flap extension reduced to 20 degrees, choice of five liquid/dry chemical dispersal systems. In 1969 Cessna shipped 14 Agwagon A ships (disassembled) to Urdaneta and Galvez, Cessna distributors in Bogota, Colombia with 12 (1970) and 8 (1971) Agwagon B completed in Colombia. The first A188A Agwagon B (c/n 18800573) is illustrated with access panels removed. Total built: 1968/69: 44 (188), 211 (A188); 1970-71: 28 (188A), 232 (A188A). Price: $24,450 (1971 Agwagon B). Engine: Continental O-470-R, 230 hp (188/188A), IO-520-D, 285 hp continuous (A188/A188A); gross weight (restricted category): 3800 pounds (188/188A), 4000 pounds (A188/A188A); maximum speed: 151 mph (A188A); wingspan: 40 feet 4 1/2 inches (standard tip); service ceiling: 11,100 feet (A188A Agwagon B).

MODEL 188B/A188B/T188C   ATC A9CE   1972-83

Cessna renamed its ag aircraft line in 1972 as the AGpickup, AGwagon C, AGtruck and AGcarryall (Model A185E). Changes were: AGtruck: 280 gallon hopper tank, electric spray valve/gatebox, wing fuel tanks, extended conical camber wingtips, 10-inch main gear and tailwheel (all standard); AGwagon C: 8.00 x 8-inch main gear tires, 10-inch tailwheel, windshield/gear wire cutters; AGpickup: lowest priced Cessna ag aircraft, 30-nozzle spray system, windshield/gear wire cutters, cable deflector, extended baggage floor. All models had the new Camber-Lift, bonded leading edge wing with airflow fences. An optional, special night operations package including two retractable spray lights and turning lights (in wingtip fairings) was available on AGwagon/AGtruck. The 1974 AGtruck gross weight

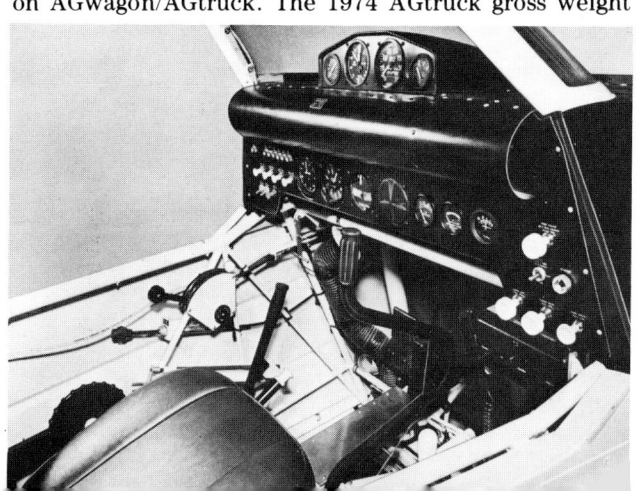

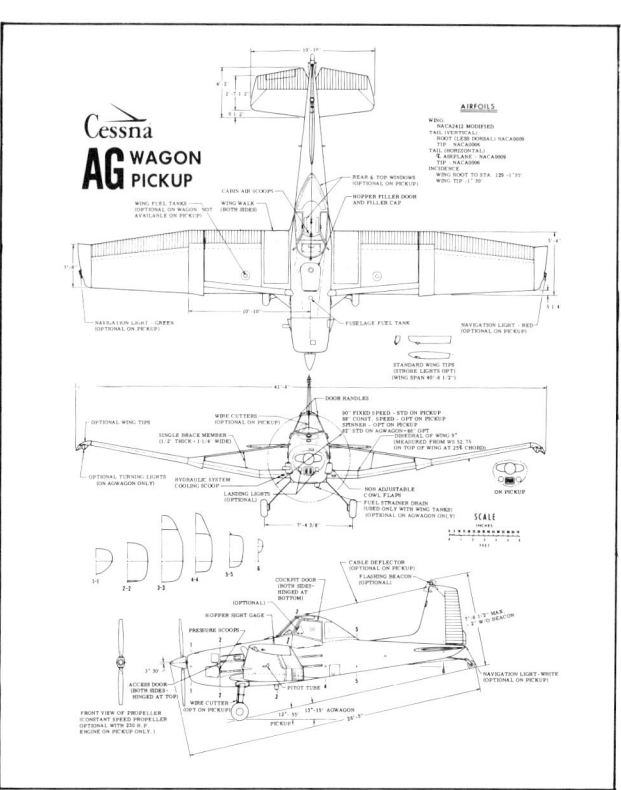

(restricted category) increased to 4200 pounds; 1975 AGwagon/AGtruck featured swing-out engine mounts, bonded equipment bay doors; 1976 models had improved dispersal systems with higher spray pressure; 1977 AGwagon fuel tanks installed in wings like AGtruck with 54 gallons capacity, relocated flap controls and new, vernier mixture control standard, optional air conditioning offered for the first time; improved, 28-volt electrical system standard on all 1978 models; Ag Husky introduced in 1979 with 310 hp turbocharged engine and 280-gallon hopper tank standard. 1980 Ag Husky with liquid dispersal equipment and optional main gear fenders shown below. Colombia built 87 AGwagon/AGtruck between 1972-75; 24 AGpickup/AGwagon were assembled in Argentina between 1972-73. Total built: 1972: 208; 1973: 334; 1974: 450; 1975: 524; 1976: 397; 1977: 301; 1978: 250; 1979: 104; 1980: 200; 1981: 135; 1982: 70. Note: Colombian production included in above figures. Price: $45,950 (1977 AGtruck). Engine: Continental O-470-R, 230 hp (A188B), O-470-S (1975 188B), IO-520-D, 285 hp continuous (A188B), TSIO-520-T, 310 hp (T188C); gross weight: 3800 pounds (188B), 4000 pounds (A188B), 4200 pounds (A188B AGtruck), 4400 pounds (T188C); maximum speed: 130 mph (Ag Husky); wingspan: 41 feet 8 inches (Ag Husky); service ceiling: 14,000 feet. (Reference Appendix A, #24) ▼

▲ **MODEL 190 PROTOTYPE 1945**
Cessna began design on a postwar, five-place cabin monoplane in 1944 with one airplane, P-780, serving as a proof-of-concept ship. Built of welded steel tubing with fabric covering and an all-metal wing, the P-780 paved the way for production airplanes that were originally called Model 180 using a 240 hp Continental W-670 radial, later redesignated by Cessna as the Model 190 in April, 1946. The second prototype built, NX41683 (c/n 7002) is illustrated with original engine cowling design surrounding a 300 hp Jacobs radial engine. Cessna's first all-metal (including flight control surfaces) airplane, it flew in October, 1945 and was completely destroyed in a crash April 11, 1946. Total built: 3. Engine: Continental W-670, 240 hp, Jacobs R-755, 300 hp; gross weight: 3350 pounds; maximum speed: 170 mph; wingspan: 36 feet two inches; service ceiling: 16,000 feet. (Reference Appendix A, #25)

▼ **MODEL 190 ATC 790 1947-53**
Big, bullish and beautiful, the 1947 Model 190 was Cessna's premier five-place ship, boasting not only good looks but good performance, cabin comfort and robust construction. 24 ST aluminum with Alclad finish was utilized for the airframe structure, with 75 gallon wing fuel tanks standard. Conventional main landing gear used chrome-vanadium spring steel with non-steerable, full-swiveling tailwheel. The cabin entry step retracted when the door was closed, a throw-over control wheel was standard and the engine was mounted on new "Dynafocal" rubber suspension points and the mount truss was hinged to swing sideward for ease of maintenance. A Hamilton-Standard two-blade, constant-speed propeller without spinner dome was also standard. To ensure adequate forward visibility while taxiing, Cessna offered a custom-made booster cushion for short pilots that was special-ordered with the airplane. Total built -1947-53: 233. Price: $14,750 (included cabin heater, two-way radio, retractable wing landing lights and basic instrument flight panel). Engine: Continental W-670 radial, 240 hp; gross weight: 3350 pounds; maximum speed: 170 mph; wingspan: 36 feet two inches; service ceiling: 16,000 feet. N9355A, a 1947 Model 190 is illustrated with optional wheel fairings. 1951 190s had a new exterior paint scheme incorporating a second stripe.

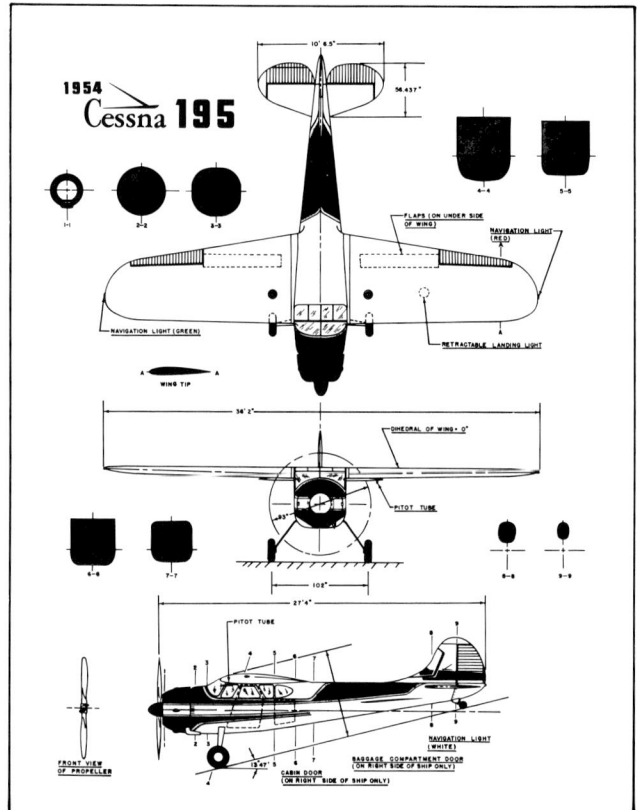

1952 Model 190 instrument panel with throwover control ▲ column. Note combination battery/magneto ignition switch.

MODEL 195/195A/195B   ATC 790   1947-54

Obtaining its Approved Type Certificate on June 12, 1947, the Model 195 featured a 300 hp Jacobs R-755, seven-cylinder radial engine. Identical to the Model 190 except for the powerplant, the 195 outsold its counterpart from 1947 to 1954, when production was halted. By March, 1950, Cessna exhausted its supply of Jacobs engines and did not renew its contract with the engine manufacturer, electing to stop production of the basic Model 195 (only until January, 1952 when the 300 hp Jacobs R-755A-2 radial was available with chrome cylinder walls/ tapered piston rings). To replace it, the company secured CAA approval to install customer-supplied Jacobs R-755-9 on 190 airframes, designated as model 195A (196 built), while Model 195B (199 built) was powered by remanufactured Jacobs R-755-B2 incorporating many improvements found in the 245 hp R-755-9 engine. Changes to the 195 airframe that occurred in the 1952 model year included a very slight reduction in vertical stabilizer area/elevator, 50% larger flaps, improved pitot tube. Total built: 1947-54: 866. Price (as of 1-53): Model 190: $16,500; Model 195A: $15,795; Model 195B: $18,750; Model 195: $23,500. Engine: Jacobs R-755-A2, 300 hp (Model 195), Jacobs R-755-9, 245 hp (Model 195A), Jacobs R-755-B2, 275 hp (Model 195B); gross weight: 3350 pounds; maximum speed (all models): above 170 mph; wingspan: 36 feet two inches; service ceiling: 17,600 feet. (Reference Appendix A, #26)

MODEL LC-126   ATC 790   1950-52

The excellent performance of Cessna's Model 195 caught the attention of the U.S. Air Force in 1949 when it needed a rugged, workhorse airplane for flight duty in the Arctic region. Uncle Sam bought 15 aircraft designated LC-126A with Federal skis and Edo floats, with deliveries occurring in January, 1950. The only differences between the military models and their civilian counterparts were an emergency escape hatch for the pilot, radio equipment and spartan interior appointments. Another batch of five LC-126B were delivered to the National Guard in 1951 and 63 LC-126C were purchased by the U.S. Army in 1952, equipped to accomodate two stretcher patients through a special, large loading door. An LC-126-CE, Air Force s/n 49-1952 is illustrated. Note pilot escape hatch on left side. LC-126 c/n were assigned concurrently with Model 195 c/n. Total built: 83. Engine: Jacobs R-755-A2, 300 hp; gross weight: 3350 pounds; maximum speed: above 175 mph; wingspan: 36 feet two inches; service ceiling: 17,600 feet. (Reference Appendix A, #27)

MODEL X-210 EXPERIMENTAL   1950-51

Proposed as a possible replacement for the Model 195, the X-210 was designed in 1949 and made its first flight in January, 1950. Principal changes from the 190-series airframe were: Continental six-cylinder, 240 hp O-470 opposed engine, square wing tips and high-lift flaps, a new empennage featuring a square vertical stabilizer, installation of tubular steel main landing gear struts. The Korean War demand for Cessna L-19 observation/liason aircraft coupled with the X-210's lack of performance improvement over the established Model 195 led to cancellation of the program in 1950. The only X-210 built (X41695) is illustrated.

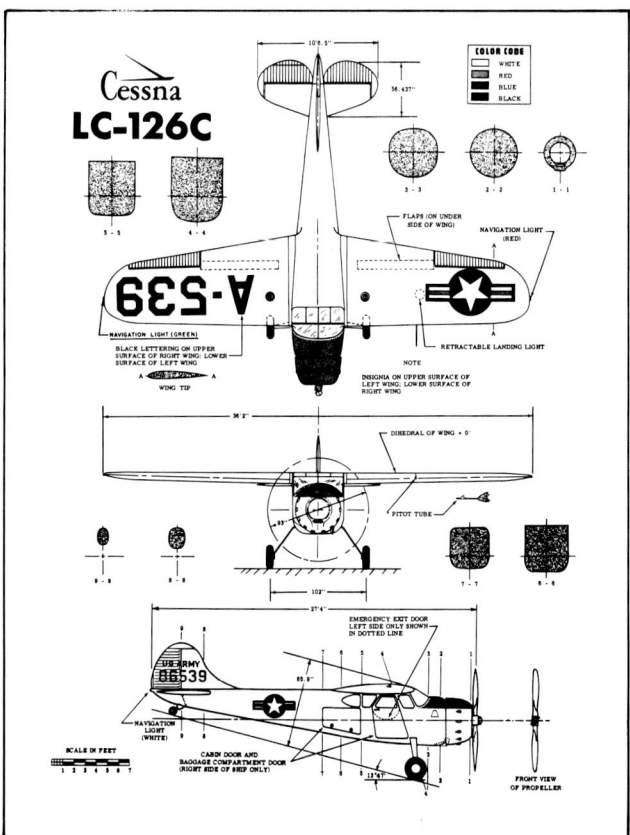

▲ MODEL 205   ATC 3A21   1963
Introduced in 1963 as a full six-seat airplane, the Model 205 possessed a hefty 1550-pound useful load, 360-degree "Omni-Vision" tinted cabin windows, electrically-operated Para-Lift flaps (40 degrees), swept vertical stabilizer, Land-O-Matic tri-cycle gear. The Model 205's carpeted cabin had 115 cubic feet of interior space, improved rocker-type switches were featured on shock-mounted instrument panel along with center-mount avionics. A vernier throttle, mixture and constant-speed propeller control were standard. Two rubber fuel cells in the wing held 65 gallons, or 84 gallons optional. Conical-camber wingtips, wheel fairings, large oil cooler, courtesy lights and third cabin door were standard equipment. Cessna marketed the 1964 model as the 205A for 1964 only. Total built: 1963: 480; 1964: 96. Price: $22,295. Engine: Continental IO-470-S, 260 hp; gross weight: 3300 pounds; maximum speed: 173 mph; wingspan: 36 feet 7 inches; service ceiling: 16,100 feet. N1802Z, an early production 205 is illustrated. Model 205 first flight: 2-8-62; pilot: R.W. Stephens.

▼ MODEL 206/U206/TU206   ATC A4CE   1964-70
Cessna created the 206-series in 1964 by taking the basic Model 205/205A (that were dropped from production after 1964), installing a 285 hp engine, beefed up fuselage structure with oversize rivets, heavy-duty brakes, useful load of 1595 pounds, pilot's seat only (standard, with three seating arrangements optional up to six seats), 42-inch double doors for ease of cargo loading that could be removed for cargo drops or for photographic work, durable, scuff-resistant, easy cleaning interior materials. Heavy-duty main gear tires, floats, skis, 300-pound capacity fuselage cargo pack, spray boom installation with 150 gallon tank and aerial ambulance version were available. Known as the "Super Skywagon", the 1966 version offered turbocharging for the first time (TU206A), three-blade constant-speed propeller and mortuary option for carrying one casket. Standard features included new, 60-ampere alternator replacing 50-ampere generator. Cessna called the U206/TU206-series Super Skywagon, Turbo (System) Super Skywagon (1964-68), Skywagon 206, Turbo-Skywagon 206 for 1969 and 1970 model years. 1966 Super Skywagon U206A is illustrated with heavy-duty tires. Total built: 1964: 275 206; 1965: 162 U206; 1966: 152 U206A, 67 TU206A; 1967: 187 U206B, 71 TU206B; 1968: 241 U206C, 77 TU206C; 1969: 157 U206D, 53 TU206D (including five built in Colombia); 1970: 107 U206E, 23 TU206E (including four built in Colombia). Price: $23,995 (1966 Model U206A). Engine: Continental IO-520-A, 285 hp continuous (206/U206/U206A), TSIO-520-C, 285 hp (1966 TU206A); gross weight: 3300 pounds (206/1965 U206), 3600 pounds (U206A/TU206A); maximum speed: 174 mph (U206A); wingspan: 36 feet 7 inches; service ceiling: 14,800 feet (U206A), 26,300 feet (TU206A).

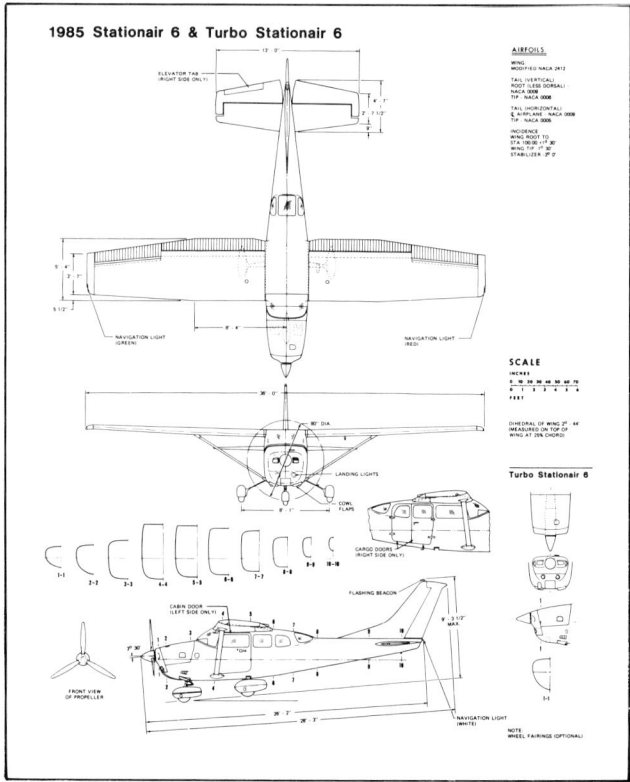

MODEL P206B   ATC A4CE   1965-70 ▶

The P206 "Super Skylane" was very similar to the Model 206/U206 but did not have the 42-inch double cargo doors of its sister ship yet retained the Model 205's six seats and third door on the left fuselage side. In 1966 turbocharging was offered as the TP206A and improvements in 1967 set the P206B/TP206B apart from earlier models: restyled interior, short-stroke nose gear oleo strut, new wheel fairings, rudder/fin tip designed to house Omni-flash beacon, revised upper cowl/nose cap, split-bus electrical system. Yearly changes were: 1968: pre-select flap control; 1969: revised glareshield with internal lighting; 1970: new, no-bulge lower cowl design, transistorized light dimming, low-mounted control wheel, press-to-reset circuit breakers. Total built: 1965 P206: 160; 1966 P206A: 114; TP206A: 32; 1967 P206B: 86; TP206B: 27; 1968 P206C: 74; TP206C: 26; 1969 P206D: 66; TP206D: 18; 1970 P206E: 36; TP206E: 8. A total of 536 P206 and 111 TP206 were built from 1965 to 1970. Price: $27,450 (P206E). Engine: Continental IO-520-A, 285 hp (P206 series), TSIO-520-C, 285 hp (TP206 series); gross weight: 3300 pounds (P206), 3600 pounds (1966 P206A/TP206A and after); maximum speed: 174 mph (P206E); wingspan: 35 feet 10 inches; service ceiling: 14,800 feet (P206E), 26,300 feet (TP206E). 1967 P206B is illustrated.

▼ MODEL U206E/G/TU206E/G   ATC A4CE   1971-86

In 1971 Cessna renamed the Super Skywagon the "Stationair", with restyled interior, revised glareshield with internal lighting, electroluminescent subpanel lighting followed in 1972 with Cessna's Camber-Lift wing, foam-padded control wheel design, enlarged baggage compartment, glareshield-mounted avionics annunciator panel, cowl-mounted taxi/landing lights; 1973: new, overhead rear cabin dome light and "Trimline" door handles, bonded cabin doors; 1974: integral cabin door armrest/handles, 1975: new wheel/brake fairings, Stationair II preferred options package, optional flush-mounted communication antenna on vertical stabilizer, removeable right lower cowl (Turbo Stationair only); 1976-77: new exterior paint schemes, energy-absorbing instrument sub panels, vernier mixture control; 1978: name changed to "Stationair 6", 28-volt electrical system, optional club seating and writing desk; 1979: revised instrument panel/control wheels; 1980-86: optional air conditioning (1986), refined interior appointments/exterior paint schemes. A 1984 Stationair 6 II is illustrated. Total built (including Turbo Stationair c/n): 1971: 113; 1972: 175 (4 in Colombia); 1973: 325 (4 in Colombia); 1974: 276 (16 in Colombia); 1975: 440 (12 in Colombia); 1976: 502 (16 in Colombia); 1977: 555 (16 in Colombia); 1978: 575 (20 in Colombia); 1979: 660; 1980: 610; 1981: 520; 1982: 258; 1983: 88; 1984: 57; 1985: 73. Price: $111,400 (1986 Stationair 6). Engine: Continental IO-520-F, 285 hp (Stationair/Stationair 6), TSIO-520-C, 285 hp (1971-76), TSIO-520-M, 310 hp (five minutes) (1977-86);

1968 Model U206 Super Skywagon instrument panel. ▲

1976 TU206F Turbo Stationair instrument panel with optional standby altimeter. ▲

gross weight: 3600 pounds; maximum speed: 156 knots (optional wheel fairings installed on 1986 Stationair 6); wingspan: 36 feet (1986 Stationair 6); service ceiling: 14,800 feet; 27,000 feet (1986 Turbo Stationair 6).

MODEL 207/SKYWAGON 207/T207
ATC A16CE   1969

Cessna introduced its biggest single-engine airplane to date with the 1969 debut of the powerful, rugged utilitarian Skywagon 207. Based on the Model U206C cabin section, wing, lift struts and basic empennage (with strengthened spar fittings), the Herculean 207 held six full sized adults in its 155.5 cubic foot cabin. Cessna engineers modified the U206E by adding an 18-inch stretch forward of the firewall and a 30-inch stretch aft of the rear doorpost, permitting a seventh passenger seat and additional baggage area not available in the Model 206 series. The Model 207 utilized the left front door and double cargo doors of the P206C and included an extra cabin window for 360-degree Omni-Vision. The wing spar featured six-bolt fuselage attach fittings instead of the 206s' four-bolt system. 206 nose cap bulge was eliminated. Tapered tubular steel gear struts and an entirely new nose wheel steering system was installed. TU206C c/n TU206-0921 served as the developmental test bed for the 207, assigned experimental c/n 665. Standard features of the Model 207 were: flap pre-select control (40 degrees), split-bus electrical system, canted engine instrument cluster, new control wheels, 65-gallon fuel tanks (84 gallon optional). The T207 turbocharged version had standard 76-cubic foot oxygen cylinder with cabin outlets. Total built: 1969 207: 105 (including c/n 665), T207: 44. Price: $28,250 (Skywagon 207); gross weight: 3800 pounds; maximum speed: 168 mph; wingspan: 36 feet 7 inches; service ceiling: 13,300 feet. A 1969 Skywagon 207 is illustrated. Model T207 first flight: 5-11-68; pilot: P.R. Leckman.

MODEL 207/T207/207A SKYWAGON
ATC A16CE   1970-77

Changes for 1970-77 Skywagon 207 series included: 1970: revised control wheel design, optional shadow gray instrument panel, optional mortuary modification for single casket; 1973: larger, padded control wheels, bonded cabin doors, new glareshield, color-keyed avionics, new wheel fairings, rocker switches for lighting; 1974: integral armrest/cabin door handles, miniaturized marker beacon display, revised glareshield with audio panel annunciators, optional 28-volt electrical system; 1975: revised glareshield, flush-mounted, removeable rear cabin air outlets; 1977: energy-absorbing instrument sub panels, improved vernier mixture control, rectangular hour meter, TSIO-520-M engine with 80-inch diameter, constant-speed three-blade propeller, improved aileron control system with redesigned pulley brackets. 1973 Skywagon 207 with optional wheel fairings is illustrated. Total built: 1970 207: 32; T207: 10; 1971 207: 11, T207: 2; 1972 207: 8; T207: 2; 1973 207: 9; T207: 3; 1974 207: 29; T207: 11; 1975 207: 37; T207: 10; 1976 207: 28; T207: 20; 1977 207A: 34; T207A: 18; Price: $48,650 (1977 207A). Engine: Continental IO-520-F, 300 hp (2850 rpm, five minutes); TSIO-520-G, 300 hp (five minutes); 1977 T207A: TSIO-520-M, 310 hp (five minutes); gross weight: 3800 pounds; maximum speed: 150 knots (Skywagon 207); wingspan: 35 feet, 10 inches; service ceiling: 13,300 feet (Skywagon 207), 26,000 feet (Turbo Skywagon 207).

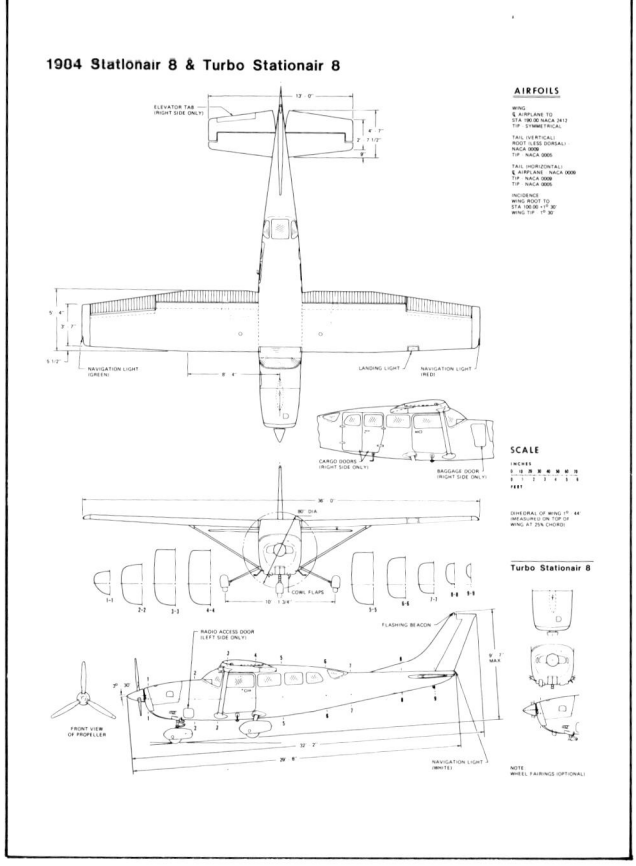

STATIONAIR 7/TURBO STATIONAIR 7
A16CE   1978-85

Continued improvements to the Model 207 series resulted in the 1978 Stationair 7 version with 28-volt electrical system standard, followed in 1979 with a new, long-hub propeller/spinner combination (required special exhaust stack extensions to meet FAR Part 36 decibel levels). For 1980, Cessna developed an eight seat arrangement and changed names again to Stationair 8, with new interior fabrics, optional 6-place club seating, refreshment center and writing table, new flap position indicator and pull-type alternator circuit breaker. 1984 improvements were: engine TBO was extended from 1400 to 1600 hours, composite, warp-resistant fuel caps, shoulder harness standard (all seats), vacuum system, attitude/heading indicators standard, copilot control wheel/rudder pedals standard. Total built: 1978 207A: 68; 1979: 80; 1980: 92; 1981: 75; 1982: 33; 1983: 4; 1984: 20; 1985: no c/n assigned. As of 1982 model year, 761 Model 207/T207 had been built. Price: $112,800 (1984). Engine: Continental IO-520-F, 285 hp (continuous), TSIO-520-M, 310 hp (2700 rpm, five minutes); gross weight: 3800 pounds; maximum speed: 150 knots (1984 Stationair 8 with optional wheel fairings); wingspan: 35 feet 10 inches; service ceiling: 13,300 feet, 26,000 feet (Turbo Stationair 8). 1983 Stationair 8 II is illustrated (note extended exhaust stacks).

1980 T207 Turbo Stationair 8 instrument panel.

MODEL T207   ATC A16CE   1976

The Argentine Army purchased five Model T207s in April, 1976 for use in tactical military maneuvers, including troop movements, reconnaisance, aerial observation and photography. All five were equipped with 300 hp (takeoff, five minutes) turbocharged Continental TSIO-520-G engines with three-blade, constant-speed propellers. Seven Argentine Army pilots ferried the T207s back to Moron Air Force Base with a final assignment to Campo De Mayo. Along with the T207 order the Argentine Army also took delivery of five T-41D (R172H) in May, 1976. The orders were placed through Cygnus, Cessna's distributor based in Buenos Aires.

1976 Turbo 207 instrument panel.

▲ MODEL 208/208A/208B CARAVAN I
ATC A37CE   1983-86

On December 9, 1982 Cessna's all-new Caravan I single-engine turboprop made its maiden flight from the Pawnee Division facility in East Wichita. Targeted directly at the charter/cargo operator, the Model 208 seats up to 14 passengers, can accomodate two D-size freight containers or hundreds of small packages. Cessna's second turboprop single-engine model (XL-19B/C were first turboprop models, developed in 1952 and 1953), Caravan I is powered by a Pratt & Whitney turboprop engine developing 600 shaft horsepower. Largest Model 208A operator is small package carrier Federal Express. A second version featuring a four-foot fuselage stretch and known as the Model 208B, flew March 3, 1986. The stretched Caravan I has a useful load of 4,273 pounds compared to the 3,777 pounds of its predecessor. Payload is 3,500 pounds contained in 450 cubic feet, including a fuselage-mounted cargo pod. N208LP, the first prototype airplane, is illustrated. Model 208 is approved for Wipline floats and amphibious-type floats beginning at 1985 c/n 20800030 and after complying with Federal Aviation Regulation 23.751. Total delivered: February, 1985 to March, 1986: 70. Price: $660,000 (1986 Caravan I). Engine: Pratt & Whitney PT6A-114, 600 shp. gross weight: 8000 pounds (1986 Caravan I), 7635 pounds (floatplane and amphibious floats); maximum speed: cruise at 10,000 feet: 183 knots (landplane), 158 knots (floatplane), 153 knots (amphibious floats); wingspan: 52 feet 1 inch; service ceiling: 27,600 feet (landplane).

▼ MODEL U-27A   ATC A37CE   1986

The Model 208A Caravan I can also serve in military configuration as the U-27A, with Cessna's military demonstrator illustrated in overall gray paint scheme. Not intended to be a front-line combat aircraft, the U-27A is designed to be a multipurpose armed forces aircraft capable of handling small group troop movements, supply and liason duties into unimproved airstrips, surveillance, medical evacuation and other military-related services. As of May, 1986 the U.S. Army is considering leasing or purchasing a Caravan I to determine its suitability for medical evacuation and control of RPV (Remotely Piloted Vehicle) aircraft. Two U-27A entered military service with the Liberian Army in 1986. Both the Caravan I and U-27A feature a standby flap motor, 28-volt electrical system, standby alternator, tubular spring steel main landing gear with inter-tube, drag link nose gear. Fuel capacity is 335 gallons in two integral (wet cell) wing tanks. Corrosion proofing is standard. Specifications/performance similar to Caravan I.

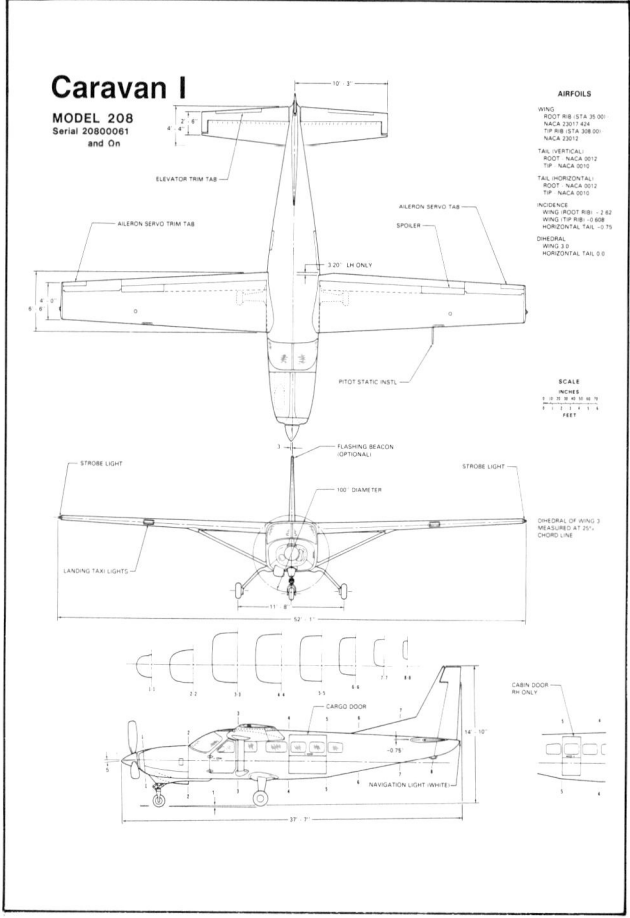

MODEL 210 PROTOTYPE 1956

Cessna's eighth addition to its ever-expanding line of business/personal airplanes was announced on April 6, 1959 as the Model 210, a single-engine, high wing, four-place ship with retractable landing gear. The first prototype, c/n 616, flew in 1957 with a second prototype, c/n 618 flying in 1959. An electro-hydraulic retraction system was fitted into the fuselage with eight gear doors covering the main/nose gear in flight. A semi-cantilever all-metal wing was utilized along with a 260 hp, fuel-injected Continental engine to give the Model 210 a solid 20 mph maximum speed advantage over the Model 182/Skylane. The 210 was the right airplane at the right time for Cessna as many pilots were ready to step up from fixed to retractable gear performance. N1296, the first flying prototype is illustrated. Prototype Model 210 constructor numbers were: c/n 616 and 618. Total built: two (1956 and 1959). Engine: Continental IO-470-E, 260 hp at 2625 rpm; gross weight: approximately 2900 pounds (varied with engineering flight test equipment/modifications); maximum speed: above 190 mph; wingspan: 36 feet two inches; service ceiling: 20,700 feet. Model 210 first flight: 2-25-57: pilot: R.L. Crawshaw.

MODEL 210   ATC 3A21   1960

Unveiled to the aviation press in August, 1959, the 210 featured Cessna's swept tail and conical-camber wingtips standard, designed to improve the spiral stability of the airplane. An engine-driven hydraulic pump provided pressure to retract cylinders with rack-and-pinion action that rotated and retracted the gear. All eight doors were priority-sequenced to open and close with the nose gear retracting forward as the main gear swung up/aft in 3 1/2 seconds. All three gear featured individual up/down locks. Manual gear extension used a hydraulic pump handle in

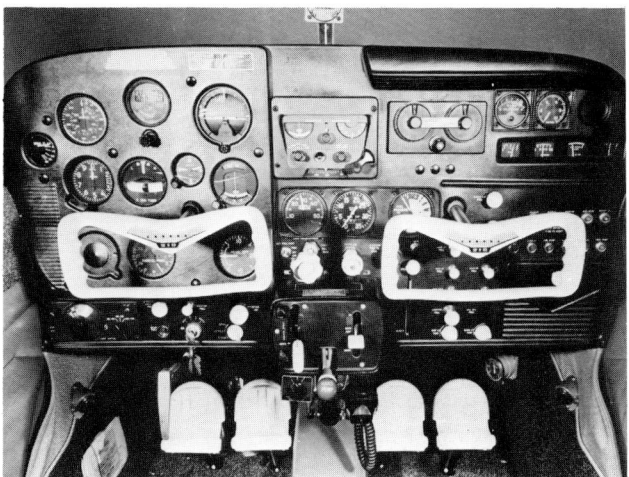

1960 Model 210 instrument panel fully equipped with gyroscopic flight instruments.

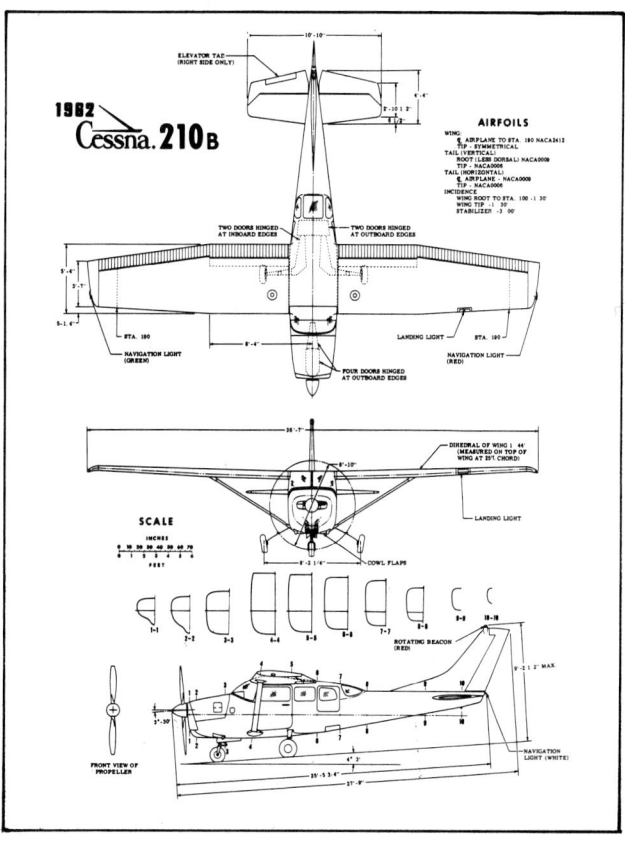

the instrument panel console with its own fluid reservoir. Flaps were also hydraulically operated. Interior room was provided for four adults. Auxiliary electric fuel pump, 35-ampere generator, landing lights, landing gear position/warning lights, vernier throttle, propeller and mixture controls, cowl flaps were standard. Total built: 577 (includes c/n 616, c/n 618). Price: $22,450. Engine: Continental IO-470-E, 260 hp; gross weight: 2900 pounds; maximum speed: 199 mph; wingspan: 36 feet five inches; service ceiling: 20,700 feet.

▲ MODEL 210A   ATC 3A21   1961

After only one year on the market, Cessna revamped its Model 210 into the 210A with a complete interior redesign including a wide selection of cabin fabrics, vinyl trim that covered previously exposed airframe structure, "Pan Lam" inserts in white plastic escutcheons, Royalite baggage compartment, new seating with "Polycloud" cushions, 3-position reclining front seats, two inches more headroom in the rear cabin and a third cabin window for greater outside viewing area. "Blend-Temp" environmental control system, key-operated magneto/start switch, simplified hydraulic controls for gear and flaps, fixed lower/split upper cowling with Cam-loc fasteners, large, external baggage door with improved key lock and door seal were standard, an autopilot and 84-gallon fuel tanks were optional, six exterior color combinations were also available. Total built: 265. Engine: Continental IO-470-E, 260 hp; gross weight: 2900 pounds; maximum speed: 199 mph; wingspan: 36 feet six inches; service ceiling: 20,700 feet. Model 210A first flight: 1-2-61; pilot: W.D. Thompson

▼ MODEL 210B/C/D/E CENTURION   ATC 3A21   1962-65

Major change for the 1962 Model 210B was Omni-Vision rear windows and restyled/enlarged cabin side windows. A Continental IO-470-S engine replaced the IO-470-E powerplant and gross weight increased to 3000 pounds. The 1964 210D was first version to bear the name "Centurion" with 3100-pound gross weight, engine change to a 285 hp Continental IO-520-A engine with durable nitrided cylinders and chrome piston rings, redesigned upper/lower cowling with a pointed propeller spinner, first-ever six-seat option (two aft seats were child seats), change from hydraulic to electrically-operated flaps with additional 8 square feet of area, needle bearings on new, wide-chord ailerons, horizontal stabilizer span increased eight inches, redesigned wheel/brake assemblies, larger capacity cabin heater, individual reading lights, aluminum rudder pedal scuff plates and black panel standard. Optional leathers, electric vertically-adjustable front seats, dual latch-top cabin storage compartments were offered for first time. Total built: 1962 210B: 246 (including prototype c/n 637); 1963 210C: 135; 1964: 290; 1965: 204. Engine: Continental IO-470-S, 260 hp (1962-63), IO-520-A, 285 hp (1964); gross weight: 3000 pounds (1962-63), 3100 pounds (1964); maximum speed: 199 mph; wingspan: 36 feet seven inches; service ceiling: 20,700 feet (1962-63), 21,000 feet (1964).

▲ MODEL 210F/T210F   ATC 3A21   1966

Turbocharging came to the Centurion in 1966 as an option on the T210F that included a complete cabin oxygen system for pilot and passengers with a 76 cubic-foot oxygen cylinder and six masks. The TSIO-520-F engine rested on semi-Dynafocal rubber mounts and exhausted through a large, single stack on the right side of the all-new cowling. A one-piece, wrap-around windshield 1/4-inch thick made its first appearance on a 210 along with 1/4-inch thick pilot window and double-pane cabin windows for decreased noise level. A 60-ampere alternator, new rotary door locks, Open-View control wheels and a six-place interior were standard with four-place interior seating, 3-blade propeller optional. Total built: 210F: 103; T210F: 197. Engine: Continental IO-520-A, 285 hp; TSIO-520-C, 285 hp; gross weight: 3,300 pounds; maximum speed: 198 mph (230 mph at 19,000 feet -T210F); wingspan: 36 feet seven inches; service ceiling: 19,900 feet (210F), 31,300 feet (T210F).

1966 Model 210F instrument panel. ▲

▲ MODEL 210G/H/J-T210G/H/J
ATC 3A21   1967-69

Major change for the Centurion series came in 1967 when a full cantilever wing became standard with the 210G/T210G. Utilizing a modified NACA 64A215 at the center tapering to a modified NACA 64A12 at the tips, the new wing featured laminar flow, 89 gallon integral (wet) fuel tanks. The wing's leading edge was positioned 4.5 inches aft of previous leading edge location, improving sideward visibility but requiring a six square-foot increase in horizontal stabilizer/elevator area because of increased need for pitch control authority under certain forward CG loadings. Other changes were: improved aerodynamic balance on ailerons, 3400 pound gross weight, foam-filled glareshield, instrument white lighting, underseat storage compartments, new fresh air outlets, canted engine instruments, fuel gauges with color-coded quantity indicators displaying standard and extended-range tank capacity, black Royalite panel. 1968 210H/T210H: "Action" control wheel optional with electric elevator trim, mic button and chart light incorporated in grip horns, metal-to-metal seat belts, flap control handle with 10, 20 and 30-degree detents. 1969 210J/T210J: redesigned, padded glareshield was the only significant model year change. Total built: 1967 210G: 118; T210G: 110; 1968 210H: 125; T210H: 85; 1969 210J: 138; T210J: 62. Price: $26,950 (210G), $31,975 (T210G). Engine: Continental IO-520-A, 285 hp (1967-68), TSIO-520-C, 285 hp (1967-68); IO-520-H, 285 hp (1969), TSIO-520-H, 285 hp (1969); gross weight: 3400 pounds; maximum speed: 200 mph (210G); wingspan: 36 feet 9 inches; service ceiling: 18,300 feet (210G).

▲ MODEL 210K/T210K   ATC 3A21   1970-71

Refinements to the very popular Centurion continued with the 1970/71 210K/T210K. Large, three-foot long picture windows were added to the aft cabin that greatly increased Omni-Vision area, new seating angle and shape improved comfort and all four seats featured articulating mechanisms. Only the pilot's seat had standard vertical adjustment. Baggage door size increased to 29 inches, redesigned gear system permitted 25% increase in cabin volume, tapered chrome vanadium tubular steel gear struts with integral brake lines replaced spring units. Useful load increased 288 pounds. A capacitance-type fuel quantity/indication system was installed for the first time. Low-mounted control wheels featured larger grip horns, a split master switch was standard and turbocharging was optional. In 1971 Cessna added the "Centurion II" preferred options package featuring full IFR avionics, dual controls, full gyro panel and most popular interior/exterior appointments. 1971 standard improvements were: ensolite-padded front doorposts, instrument subpanels and front seatbacks, foam-cushioned glareshield, fuel quantity gauges readout in pounds/gallons, black-anodized control columns with integral wiring tapes. Total built: 1970 210K: 92 (includes c/n 668 prototype), T210K: 61 (two in Colombia); 1971 210K: 94, T210K: 57 (six in Colombia). Price: $39,250 (1971 T210K). Engine: IO-520-L, 285 hp continuous (300 takeoff), TSIO-520-H, 285 hp; gross weight: 3800 pounds; maximum speed: 230 mph (19,000 feet, T210K); wingspan: 36 feet 9 inches; service ceiling: 28,500 feet (T210K). 1970 210K demonstrator is illustrated with optional three-blade propeller. Note wingtip location of landing/taxi lights.

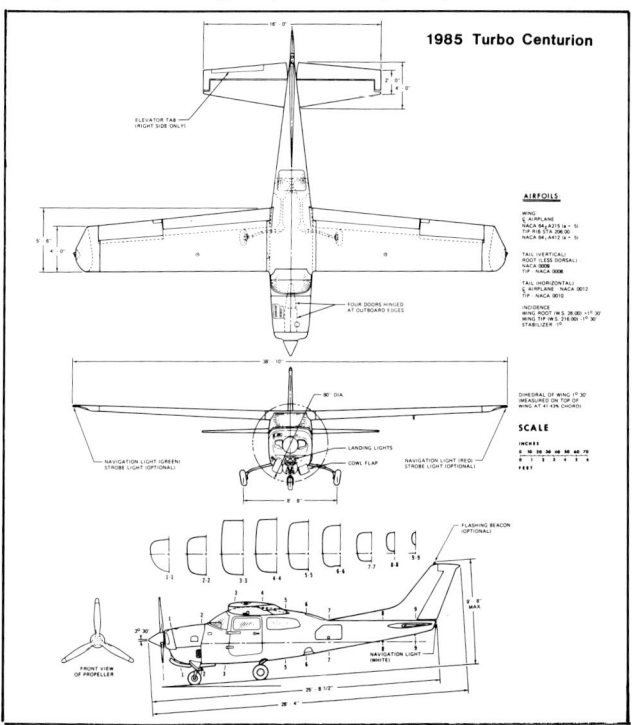

▲ MODEL 210L/M/N -T210L/M/N
ATC 3A21   1972-79

Changes to the 1972-79 Centurions were: 1972 210L/T210L: new cowl-mounted taxi/landing lights, 28-volt electrical system, aft cabin dome light panel, instrument primary scales on outside, polyurethane foam-padded/adjustable control wheels, hydro-electric gear powerpack replaced engine-driven hydraulic pump, revised gear control handle/lights, avionics audio panel in glareshield. 1973 210L/T210L: gear control handle (pull-to-move action) relocated to left instrument subpanel, bonded cabin doors; 1974 210L/T210L: deeper cushioned seats, revised cabin heating/ventilation system, integral armrest and door handles. 1975 210L/T210L: three-blade propeller standard, cabin entry step cycled with gear, removeable lower right cowl panel on T210L only. 1976 210L/T210L: aileron gap seals, restyled fin/rudder tip, instrument panel featured basic "T" grouping, primary airspeed scale in knots, new priority valve for gear door retraction sequencing, bonded baggage door, optional windshield anti-ice plate. 1977 210L/T210L: avionics master switch, improved cabin ventilation, TSIO-520-R (T210M) engine. 1978 210M/T210M: glareshield/instrument panel with relocated rocker switches and provision for weather radar screen, redesigned gear control handle/lights, fuel gauges relocated to floor console. 1979 210N/T210N: alternator/regulator unit with low-volt indicator, fuselage main gear wells eliminated doors. Total built: 1972-78 210/T210: 3452 (including 20 T210 in Colombia); 1979 210N/T210N: 685. As of the 1978 model year, 6412 Model 210s had been built, with 3869 210 and 2543 T210 comprising the total. Price: $65,950 (1977 T210M). Engine: Continental IO-520-L, 285 hp (300 hp takeoff), TSIO-520-H, 285 hp (1972-76), TSIO-520-R, 285 hp (310 hp takeoff, 1977); gross weight: 3800 pounds (1972-78 210), 4000 pounds (1979 T210); maximum speed: 204 knots (17,000 feet, T210N); wingspan: 36 feet 9 inches; service ceiling: 27,000 feet (T210N).

▼ MODEL 210N/R-T210N/R ATC 3A21 1980-86
The 1980 210N featured 10 degrees of flap extension up to 160 knots, improved door latches, optional air conditioning offered for the first time in a Model 210, new flap position indicator, optional standby generator (T210 only), instrument panel finished in burl, black or shadow gray finish. By 1985 the 210N featured a redesigned cowling, pressurized magnetos that weighed three pounds less per unit; offered dual alternators and vacuum pumps as optional equipment, 165-knot gear extension speed and improved cabin environmental systems. In 1985, horizontal stabilizer/elevator span increased by three feet for improved pitch control/longitudinal stability, fiberglass wingtips meeting FAR Part 23 requirements for lightning strike protection, larger cowl flaps. The T210R features single-stage turbocharger intercoolers, new cowl and can be equipped for flight in icing conditions with wing/tail boots. Total built: 1980-1984: 210N/T210N: 1980: 495; 1981: 400; 1982: 237; 1983: 49; 1984: 74; 1985: 210R/T210R: 51. Price: $165,750 (T210R). Engine: Continental IO-520-L, 285 hp (300 hp takeoff), TSIO-520-R (1980-85) 310 hp (takeoff), TSIO-520-CE, 325 hp (1985); gross weight: 3800 pounds (1980-84), 3850 pounds (1985); 4000 pounds (T210N/R, 1980-84), 4100 pounds (1985); maximum speed: 225 knots at 20,000 feet (T210R); wingspan: 36 feet 9 inches; service ceiling: 29,000 feet (T210R). A 1986 T210R is illustrated.

▲ MODEL P210N ATC 3A21 1978-84
Cessna created a new breed of Centurion in 1978 when it announced the pressurized P210N; the world's only pressurized single-engine airplane at that time. Cabin windows were redesigned to semi-oval shape and reduced in size, with a sliding window on the left cabin doors only and one emergency exit on the right side. Double heat exchangers provided cabin environmental comfort and a special high-capacity turbocharger handled engine manifold pressure requirements as well as pressurizing the cabin to 12,000 feet at an airplane altitude of 23,000 feet. Higher flap extension speeds were permitted in 1980 (10 degrees up to 160 knots), new flap position indicator and three panel finishes. Total built: 1978: 150; 1979: 235; 1980: 205; 1981: 170; 1982: 51; 1983: 22; 1984: none. Engine: Continental TSIO-520-P, (1978-81), 310 hp (takeoff); TSIO-520-AF (1982-84), 310 hp (takeoff); gross weight: 4000 pounds; maximum speed: 237 knots (17,000 feet); wingspan: 36 feet 9 inches; maximum operating altitude: 23,000 feet. A 1980 P210N is illustrated with optional wing-mounted weather radar. Model P210N first flight: 10-1-76; pilot: L. R. Ikerd

▼ MODEL P210R ATC 3A21 1985-86
Cessna engineers improved the P210's high altitude performance, engine and fuel systems and introduced the 1985 P210R with two, single-stage intercoolers that reduced air temperature coming from the turbocharger's compressor before sending it to the combustion chamber, reducing cylinder head temperatures. Very large cowl flaps were required to handle ground/low airspeed cooling requirements with the right side stainless steel cowl flap acting as an extractor plenum for exhaust airflow when closed. Other changes were: horizontal stabilizer/elevator span increased three feet, (eliminating previous aileron/rudder interconnect, bobweight and downsprings used on the 1978-84 P210N), new, FAR Part 23-approved (lightning protection) fiberglass wingtips for less drag and improved roll-damping at stall break, higher gross weight, 325 hp TSIO-520-CE engine, revised instrument panel with internally illuminated instruments for improved lighting. Total built: 1985 ; 31. Price: $235,200 (1986 P210R). Engine: Continental TSIO-520-CE, 325 hp; gross weight: 4100 pounds; maximum speed: 225 knots (20,000 feet); wingspan: 38 feet 8 inches; maximum operating altitude: 25,000 feet. 1986 P210R is illustrated.

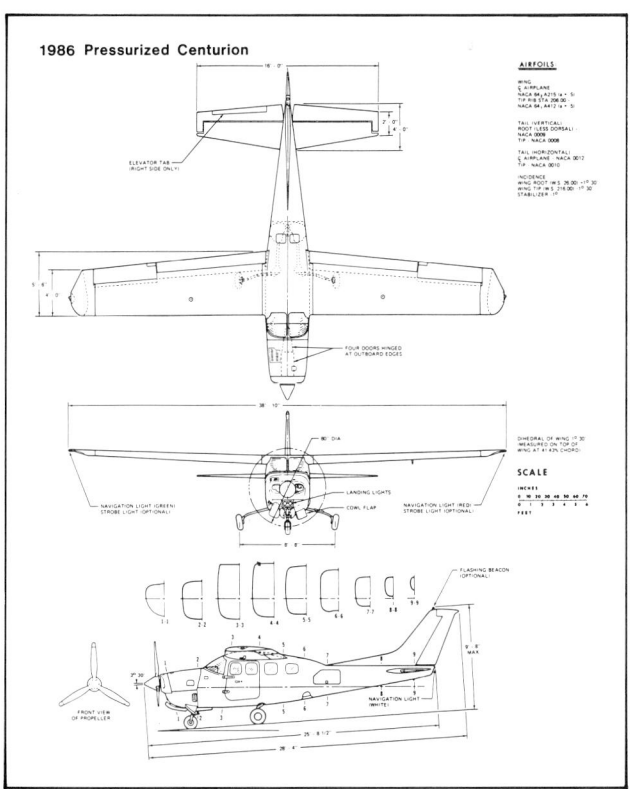

1976 turbocharged T210L instrument panel. ▲

1980 Turbo Centurion II instrument panel with optional ▲ weather radar display.

▲   Model 303   PROTOTYPE   1978

Cessna entered the light multi-engine trainer market with the experimental Model 303, first flown February 15, 1978 on a 54-minute flight by test pilot Bruce Barrett. The 303 was designed to compete against the Beech Model 76 Duchess, Piper Seminole and Grumman American's GA-7 Cougar. Powered by two 160 hp engines with constant-speed propellers, Cessna's 303 utilized the new GA(W)-1 airfoil that incorporated supercritcal wing technology but was modified by Cessna with 16% thickness at the root and 12% thickness at the wingtips. The 303's fuselage was also of bonded construction. Flight testing progressed smoothly with the prototype ship, c/n 687 (illustrated) during evaluation in the winter of 1978. Engine: two Lycoming 0-360-A, 160 hp; gross weight: 3,600 pounds; maximum speed: 202 mph; wingspan: 32 feet 11 inches; service ceiling: approximately 18,000 feet.

▼   MODEL T303 CRUSADER
              ATC A34CE   1982-84

Cessna's Model 303 was transformed into the Model T303 "Clipper" in 1979, the first of a new generation of Cessna twins designed to replace the venerable Model 310 and Model 337 Skymaster. With a change to six seats and turbocharging, the Model 303 Prototype Clipper (c/n 694) made its first flight on October 17, 1979 with Tom Wallis piloting and a second prototype, c/n 695 flew in 1980. Named "Crusader" in 1981, Cessna's first counter-rotating-engine light twin won its ATC on August 24, 1981 and the #1 Crusader rolled off the Pawnee Division assembly line on June 15, 1981 with initial deliveries in the 1982 model year. Standard features on the 1982 T303 Crusader included: cruciform empennage design, trailing beam landing gear, camber-lift wing center-section, taxi light, EGT gauge, dual controls, ground service plug, three-blade propellers. 1984 Crusader options were air conditioning, cabin stereo, equipment for flight into icing conditions, 43" x 56" cargo door/entry door and a yaw damper control system was standard equipment. Total built: 1982: 167; 1983: 71; 1984: 57; 1985: no c/n assigned. Price: $278,450 (1984). Engine: two Teledyne Continental TSIO-520-AE (left), LTSIO-520-AE (right), 250 hp; gross weight: 5150 pounds; maximum speed: 216 knots (18,000 feet); wingspan: 38 feet 10 inches; maximum operating altitude: 25,000 feet; single-engine service ceiling: 13,000 feet.

MODEL 305   ATC 3A14   1950

In 1949, the U.S. Army needed a small, maneuverable, two-seat airplane that could perform liason duties and direct battlefield artillery from the air. Cessna's Military Contract Representative Derby Frye learned of the army's intentions to buy off-the-shelf Piper L-4 ships, obtained a copy of the preliminary design requirements in September, 1949 and contacted Cessna's chief engineer Jerry Gerteis. They learned that the ship had to takeoff and land in less than 600 feet and weigh no more than 1200 pounds. Cessna decided to design an airplane tailored for the mission and with only 18 engineers launched into the project with full force. Using a new fuselage, Model 170 wings with new, high-lift, single-slotted flaps with 60 degrees extension to permit short takeoff/landing performance, Model 195 empennage and new gear/engine mount structures, the Model 305 made its first flight only 90 days from inception. Test pilot Hank Waring flew the ship to Wright Field for the fly-off competition held by the air force and Derby Frye flew it to Fort Bragg for army evaluation. Despite being heavier than its Temco, Piper and Taylorcraft opponents, the 305 won and 418 ships were ordered initially. Designated L-19 by the military, Cessna's first Model 305, N41694 (c/n 601) is illustrated soon after completion. Total built: one. Engine: Continental O-470-13, 210 hp; maximum speed: 115 mph; wingspan: 36 feet. (Reference Appendix A, #28)

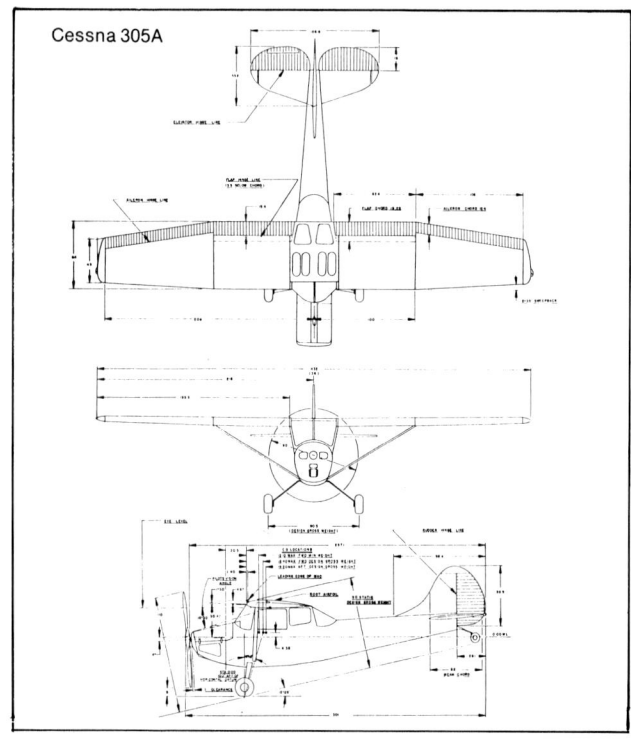

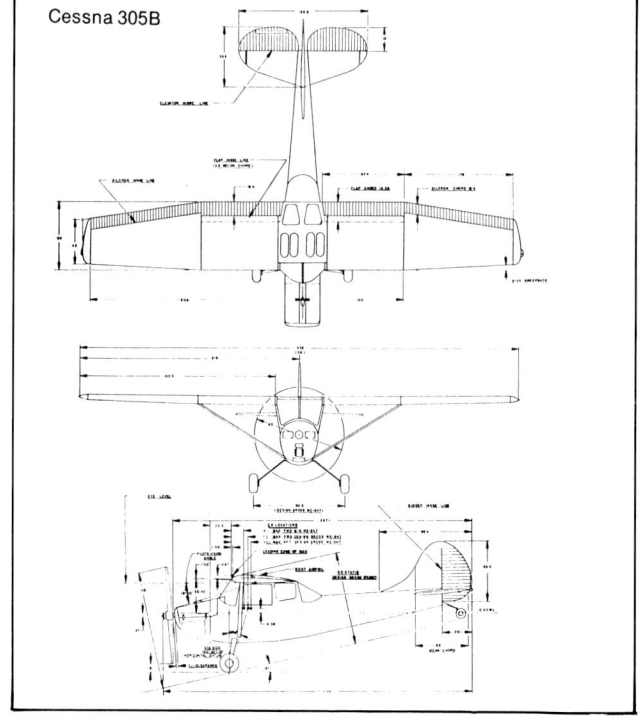

▲ MODEL 305/L-19   ATC 3A14   1950-63
Korean War hostilities caused Cessna to accelerate L-19 production with 100 L-19A ships in Korea by January, 1951. Known officially as "Birddog" by June, 1951, the tough little Cessna quickly won the respect and admiration of the pilots who flew it over the battlefront. 2400 L-19A were built between 1950-54, the Navy ordered 60 as OE-1 (identical to L-19A except for exterior paint), 66 L-19A-IT instrument trainers were delivered to the U.S. Army forces in 1953. Total built: 1950-63: 3399 (including prototype c/n 601 and four commercial Model 305). Engine: Continental O-470, 210 hp; gross weight: 2400 pounds (varied with equipment installed/military use); maximum speed: 115 mph; wingspan: 36 feet. U.S. Army L-19E illustrated. (Reference Appendix A, #29)

▲ MODEL XL-19B/C EXPERIMENTAL   1952-53
Working with Boeing and the U.S. Army, Cessna developed the XL-19B with a 210 shp turboprop engine installed in a standard L-19A, the combination making its first flight in November, 1952. Cessna pilot Bill Thompson later established an altitude record (second weight classification) of 37,063 feet with the XL-19B on July 16, 1953. The XL-19C was an USAF test project for the Continental-built French Turbomeca Artouste I of 260 shp and first flew on September 1, 1953. A second XL-19C flew on June 25, 1954 and both ships were flown from Cessna Field until 1955 when they were reconverted to L-19 status. The XL-19B (illustrated) was destroyed in crash after the engine failed at altitude and the pilot made a forced landing. Total XL-19-series built: three.

MODEL 308 EXPERIMENTAL   1951
Cessna designed the four-place Model 308 in answer to an army proposal for an airplane capable of performing as an aerial ambulance, light cargo or observation aircraft. The army intended to buy de Havilland's "Beaver", but gross weight restrictions prevented the purchase. Cessna forged ahead with its proposed 308 but continuing development problems with the Lycoming powerplant slowed the program down. In 1952 the army was permitted to buy the Beaver after weight restrictions were lifted, putting the Model 308 out of immediate contention for a government contract. Despite this setback, Cessna continued to develop the airplane and demonstrated it to the army at Fort Bragg in the spring of 1953 but to no avail. The 308 returned to Cessna, was disassembled and placed in storage. Model 308 first flight was Tuesday, July 31, 1951 with test pilot Bill Thompson at the controls. All-metal and much larger than the L-19/O-1 series, the 308 utilized high-lift flaps, six-foot augmentor tubes for engine noise reduction that were eventually replaced by cowl flaps; wrap-around cabin windows for visibility, conventional landing gear, Hamilton Standard constant-speed propeller, 1000-pound payload with 800 statute mile range. The only Model 308 built (c/n 603) is illustrated in special paint scheme applied before Fort Bragg flight demonstrations. Total built: one. Engine: Lycoming GSO-580, 375 hp; gross weight: 4200 pounds; wingspan: 47 feet. ▼

▼ MODEL 309A/B/C EXPERIMENTAL   1951-55
Cessna participated in BLC (Boundary Layer Control) research from 1951 to 1955 in conjunction with Wichita University and the U.S. Navy. A Model 170A was used for these tests, with its stock fuselage modified to house a small gas turbine that blew air over the wing; 309A utilized an engine-driven electric generator to operate large fans in the wings for blowing air; 309B/C featured dry chemicals that generated gaseous airflow across the ailerons/flaps. First flights: 309: 1951; 309B: 1953; 309C: 1954. The Model 309B is illustrated. Note drooped ailerons, secondary outboard flaps. Model 309A first flight: 2-18-52; pilot: Hank Waring

▲   MODEL 310 PROTOTYPE   1953

Cessna test pilot Hank Waring took the first Model 310 into the air on Saturday, January 3, 1953 for a 30-minute flight. The sleek, all-metal twin-engine ship represented a new beginning for Cessna that had actually started in 1951 when the company realized that many pilots wanted and needed a modern, light, multi-engine airplane. Cessna's first twin since the "Bobcat" of World War II, the 310 was conceived as a fast, five-place airplane with a comfortable cabin and twin-engine reliability. After a design study conducted from May to July, 1951, an engineering mockup and flying prototype were built. When the first 310 flew that January day, there was nothing else like it in the sky. Flight testing progressed rapidly with the first prototype, c/n 606, N41699, serving as a modification testbed and a second prototype, c/n 607, N37879 (illustrated) assigned to an accelerated 1000-hour service test program. Total built: two. Engine: two Continental O-470, 225 hp; gross weight: 4600 pounds. wingspan: 36 feet one inch; length: 27 feet one inch; height: 10 feet two inches.

▼   MODEL 310   ATC 3A10   1954-57

After receiving its ATC in March, 1954, the first production Model 310s began coming off the line in April with initial deliveries in May. Standard equipment included: steerable nose wheel, split-type flaps, Stewart-Warner combustion heater for cabin heat, shock-mounted instrument panel, constant-speed, full-feathering propellers, two wing tip tanks holding 100 gallons useable fuel, 28-volt electrical system, tri-cycle landing gear with electrical extension/retraction. Total built: 1954: 32; 1955: 226; 1956/57: 321. Engine: two Continental O-470-B, 240 hp; gross weight: 4600 pounds; maximum speed: over 220 mph; wingspan: 36 feet; service ceiling: 20,000 feet; single-engine: 7,500 feet. A 1957 Model 310 is illustrated.

▼   MODEL 310B/C   ATC 3A10   1957-59

The Model 310B (Model 310A was USAF L-27A/U-3A) featured a redesigned instrument panel, retractable cabin double-step, optional 30-gallon auxiliary fuel tanks, eight exterior color choices and three interior colors, 100-pound gross weight increase. For 1959, the Model 310C featured fuel-injected engines and a 130-pound gross weight increase. Total built: 310B: 228; 310C: 262 (including prototypes c/n 623/629); Price: $59,950 (310B). Engine: two Continental O-470-M, 240 hp (310B); IO-470-D, 260 hp (310C); maximum speed: 242 mph (310C); wingspan: 36 feet; service ceiling: 21,300 feet; single-engine: 7700 feet. N5350A, a 1959 Model 310C is illustrated. Note: Sky King's "Song Bird II" was 1958 310B, N5348A c/n 35548.

▲ MODEL 310D ATC 3A10 1960

The 1960 Model 310D featured the Flight-Sweep swept tail, fuel injected engines for the first time, non-congealing oil cooler, aileron/rudder interconnect system, improved engine muffler design, new fuel strainer drain handles in nacelles, removeable floorboards for control rigging/inspections, flush-mounted wing auxiliary fuel tank caps, gear door edge seals reduced noise, propeller/wing/tail de-icing equipment optional for the first time and five interior seating arrangments were available, including a two-place divan. Total built: 268; Note: 224 310D built at Pawnee Division then production shifted to Wallace Division plant in west Wichita where 44 310D were completed. Engine: two Continental IO-470-D, 260 hp; gross weight: 4830 pounds; maximum speed: 242 mph; wingspan: 36 feet; service ceiling: 21,300 feet; single-engine: 7700 feet. N34262 (c/n 623) illustrated was 310D prototype, later became 1963 320A prototype with same c/n and registration numbers. Note: Sky King's "Song Bird III" was 1960 310D, N6817T, c/n 39117.

▲ MODEL 310F ATC 3A10 1961

Cessna added a third, double-pane cabin window on the 310F, gave a sharp, new style to the fuselage nose cap and propeller spinners, changed to a three-position starter/magneto switch, improved cabin heating and added more comfortable front seats. 310F was the first 310 to be built at the new Military Aircraft Division factory built by Cessna on the west side of Wichita. Total built: 156. Engine: two Continental IO-470-D, 260 hp; gross weight: 4830 pounds; maximum speed: 242 mph; wingspan: 36 feet; service ceiling: 21,300 feet; single-engine: 7700 feet.

▼ MODEL 310G ATC 3A10 1962

Only major change for the 310G was new, canted wing tip tanks mounted at a 30 degree angle, improving lateral and directional stability and the airplane's overall appearance, higher gross weight, 155-pound payload increase, improved landing gear air-oil struts for softer landing/taxi operations, six more inches of useable cabin space enabled a fifth seat to easily accomodate an adult; restyled instrument panel/glareshield. Total built: 156. Engine: two Continental IO-470-D, 260 hp; gross weight: 4990 pounds; maximum speed: 244 mph; wingspan: 37 feet six inches; service ceiling: 23,600 feet; single-engine: 10,800 feet.

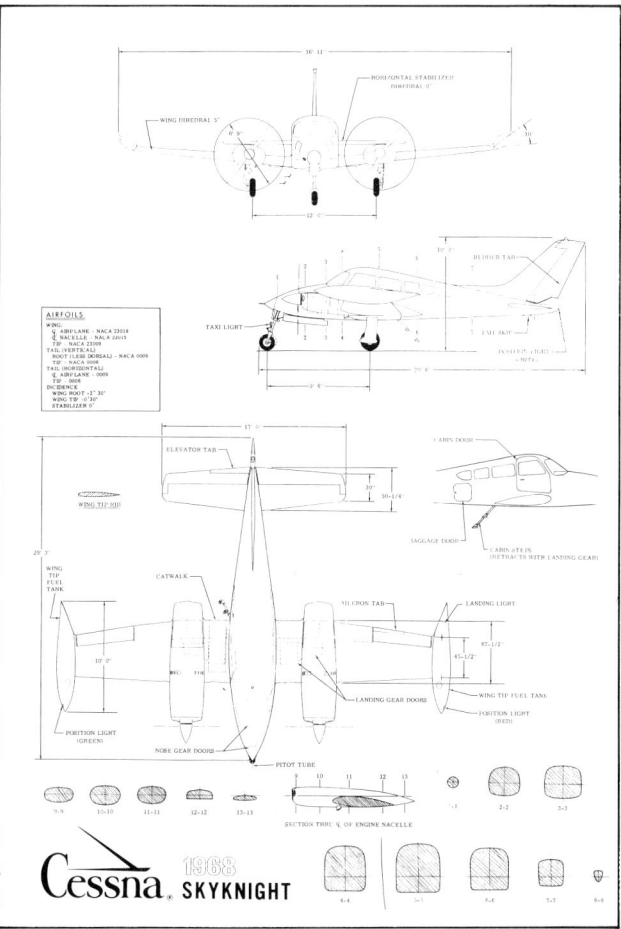

1960 Model 310D instrument panel. ▲

▲ MODEL 310H/I/J   ATC 3A10   1963-65
Significant improvements were made to the systems, interior and styling of the 1963-65 310s. A summary of changes includes: 1963 310H: 110-pound gross weight increase, aft CG limit increased from 32.5% MAC to 33.5% MAC for more flexible loading/interior configurations, Teleflex engine control cables, two aft cabin fresh air vents, propeller unfeathering accumulators optional for first time; 1964 310I: installation of an elevator bobweight improved static/dynamic longitudnal stability, removeable lower cowl panels, Janitrol 35,000 BTU combustion heater, new, nacelle baggage lockers, exhaust augmentor tubes replaced cowl flaps, flap extension reduced from 40 degrees to 35 degrees for improved balked landing performance, a full six-seat cabin, open-view control wheels, lightweight McCauley propellers; 1965 310J: redesigned engine cowlings, landing light relocated from underwing to left tip tank fairing (right light optional), new oxygen system with individual outlets, optional heated windshield. Total built: 1963: 148; 1964: 200; 1965: 200. Price: $62,950 (310I). Engine: two Continental IO-470-D, 260 hp (1963); IO-470-U, 260 hp (1964-65); gross weight: 5100 pounds; maximum speed: 238 mph (310J); wingspan: 37 feet six inches; service ceiling: 20,300 feet; single-engine: 7500 feet.

▼ MODEL 310K   ATC 3A10   1966
Model 411-type ailerons and 411 aft fairing were incorporated into the 310K along with a new wing trailing edge between aileron and nacelle that improved overall low speed control and reduced lateral control forces. New, one-piece aft cabin windows, pilot's storm window, a remote avionics access panel on both sides of the nose section, baggage door relocated further aft permitting loading without moving rear seats forward, glareshield and instrument subpanels redesigned for easier pilot operation. Total built: 245. Engine: two Continental IO-470-V, 260 hp; gross weight: 5200 pounds; maximum speed: 237 mph; wingspan: 36 feet 11 inches; service ceiling: 19,900 feet; single-engine: 6850 feet.

▲ MODEL 310L/N   ATC 3A10   1967-68
The 310L/N incorporated further improvements to the 310 line, including: 1967 310L: redesigned cabin entry step, Model 411-type fuel selector valve with integral strainer/drain, 50 ampere alternators, one-piece windshield without center post, modified Model 411-type main gear struts improved ground handling, takeoff and landing characteristics; Model 411-type gear retraction motor and redesigned gear retract mechanism permitted 160 mph gear extension. 1968 310N: redesigned instrument panel permitting 16.8 square inch increase in panel area, basic flight instruments moved in front of pilot, engine instruments moved to right side, center panel accomodated avionics, instrument subpanel redesigned to accomodate subsystem switches, larger glareshield contained avionics audio panel, external lighting and de-ice controls. Ram air intakes located on inboard wing leading edge routed engine intake air to fuel injection throttle body, replacing cowling intakes. Forward wing locker fuel tanks available for the first time. 1967 310L (c/n 664) illustrated. Total built: 1967: 208; 1968: 198. Engine: two Continental IO-470-V, 260 hp (1967); IO-470-VO, 260 hp (1968); gross weight: 5200 pounds; maximum speed: 237 mph; wingspan: 36 feet 11 inches; service ceiling: 19,900 feet; single-engine: 6850 feet.

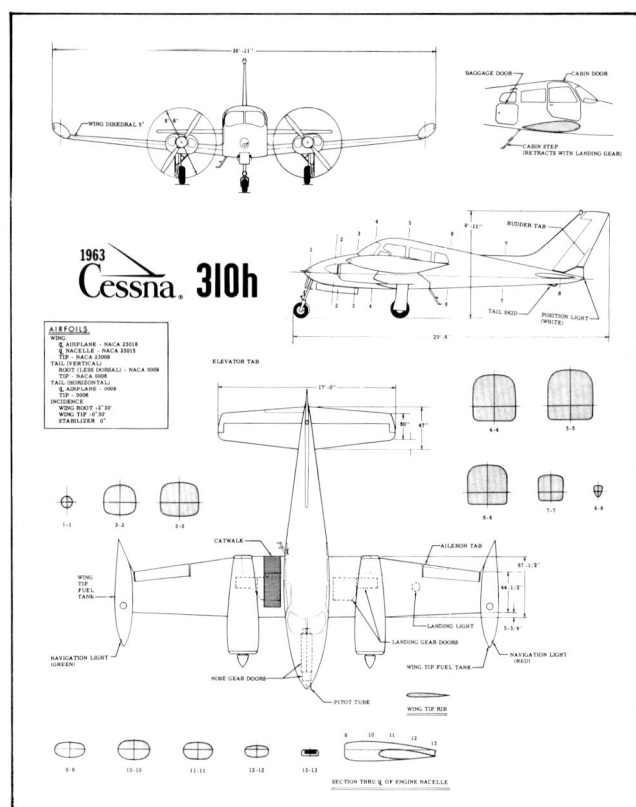

▲ MODEL 310P/TURBO-SYSTEM 310P
ATC 3A10 1969

Turbocharging came to the 310 in 1969 with introduction of the Turbo-System 310P, featuring fully automatic control of the exhaust-driven turbocharger for sea level horsepower up to 16,000 feet. Other new improvements were: nose gear angle changed to near vertical to improve ground handling and tight turns, circuit breakers canted upward for easier readability, ventral fairing/tail cone improved directional stability, nacelle-mounted engine cooling louvers (Turbo-System 310P only), pre-select flap control, new volt/ammeter with volt/amp selector switch. Total built: 240 (by 1969, Cessna had produced over 3,000 310s). Price: $65,950 (Turbo-System 310P). Engine: two Continental IO-470-VO, 260 hp (310P); TSIO-520-B, 285 hp (Turbo-System 310P); gross weight: 5200 pounds (310P), 5400 pounds (Turbo-System 310P); maximum speed: 235 mph (Turbo-System 310P); wingspan: 36 feet 11 inches; service ceiling: 28,600 feet; single-engine: 18,100 feet (Turbo-System 310P). A 1969 310P is illustrated.

▼ MODEL 310Q/TURBO 310Q
ATC 3A10 1970-74

Further refinements in the 310 series for the early '70s were features of the 310Q version. Starting with the 1970 model, changes were: 1970: 100-pound gross weight increase, easier-to-read instrumentation, capacitance-type fuel quantity system. 1972: new, one-piece rear cabin window and larger windshield, higher rear cabin ceiling, low-mounted glareshield and Sky-Gray instrument panel finish, air conditioning available for the first time. 1973/74: removeable access panel for gear motor permitted inspection/service without removing seats/floorboards; 310 II preferred options package with IFR avionics (1974), abrasion-resistant white paint applied to landing gear struts. Total built: 1970: 120; 1971: 91; 1972: 145; 1973: 245; 1974: 260. Price: $69,950 (1971 310Q). Engine: two Continental IO-470-VO, 260 hp; TSIO-520-B, 285 hp (Turbo 310Q); gross weight: 5300 pounds; 5500 pounds (Turbo-System 310Q and Turbo 310Q); maximum speed: 205 knots (310Q); wingspan: 36 feet 11 inches; service ceiling: 19,500 feet; single-engine: 6680 feet (310Q). 1974 Turbo 310 II illustrated.

▲ MODEL 310R   ATC 3A10   1975-80

Entering its 21st year of continous production, the 1975 310R featured a completely new nose section that could accomodate up to 350 pounds of remote avionics and baggage while improving the 310's overall appearance. Access to the 21 cubic-foot nose baggage compartment was through a safety-catch door on the left side. 285 hp engines and three-blade propellers were standard on the 1975 Model 310R. For 1976, improved wheels/brakes, stronger cabin door/restraint system were featured while the 1977 310R had durable polyurethane exterior paint, improved ventilation system, expanded-capacity circuit breaker panel as standard equipment. 1978-80 310R offered leather seats as an option and new design control wheels graced the gray instrument panel. Total built: 1975: 330; 1976: 235; 1977: 204; 1978: 234; 1979: 190; 1980: 99. Price: $138,500 (1977 Model 310 II). Engine: two Continental IO-520-M, 285 hp (1975-78), IO-520-MB 285 hp (1979-80); TSIO-520-B, 285 hp (Turbo 310R, 1975-78); TSIO-520-BB, 285 hp (1979-80); gross weight: 5500 pounds; maximum speed: 207 knots (1980 310R); wingspan: 36 feet 11 inches; service ceiling: 19,750 feet; single-engine: 7400 feet (1980 310R). A 1975 310 II is illustrated.

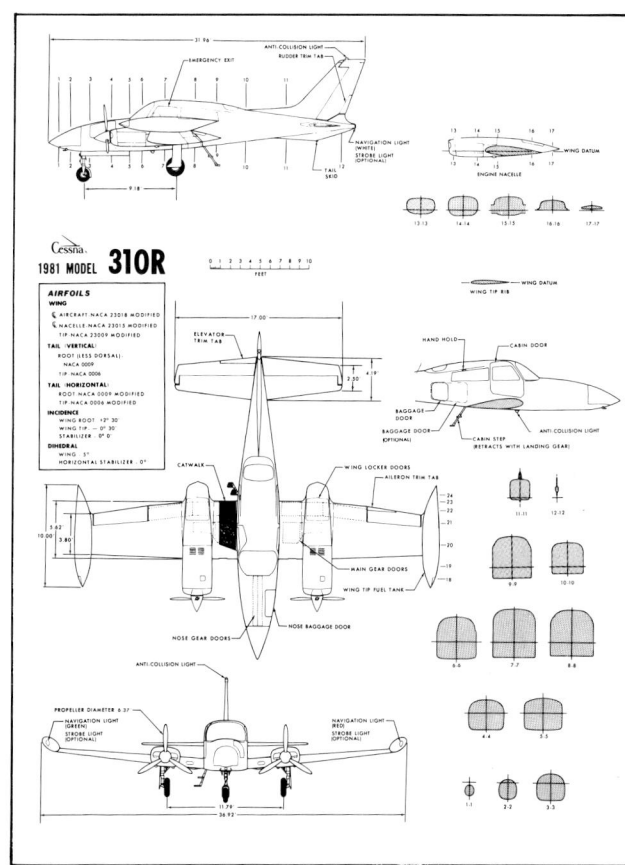

1969 Model 310P instrument panel.

1980 Model 310R instrument panel with weather radar display.

MODEL 310R   ATC 3A10   1981

The 1981 Cessna 310R represented the zenith of development and refinement that had been applied to the 310 series in more than a quarter century of production, but 1981 was the last year for the venerable light twin after 5447 commercial and military models had been built since 1953. Advanced materials technology, higher costs and sales competition from Cessna's own twin-engine Model 340 and upcoming T303 Crusader combined with declining 310 customer interest to end production. In May, 1981 the last Model 310, N6834X, c/n 310R2140, rolled off the line. Total built in 1981 model year: 40. Engine: two Continental IO-520-MB, 285 hp (310R); TSIO-520-BB, 285 hp (Turbo 310R); gross weight: 5500 pounds; maximum speed: 237 knots (16,000 feet, Turbo 310R); wingspan: 36 feet 11 inches; service ceiling: 27,400 feet; 17,200 feet (Turbo 310R). N3313M, a 1981 Model 310R is illustrated.

MODEL L-27A/U-3   ATC 3A10   1957-58

When the U.S. Air Force held its 1956 competition for a commercially-produced light multi-engine airplane suitable for general liason and light cargo missions, the Cessna Model 310 was declared the winner. 160 were purchased between 1957 and 1958. Originally designated L-27A by the USAF and Model 310A by Cessna, deliveries began in May, 1957 and the first batch of 80 ships were in air force hands by December. Redesignated U-3A in 1958, a second group of 80 airplanes were ordered that year and deliveries were completed between May and November, 1958. All 160 L-27A/U-3A were produced at Cessna's Pawnee Division factory in east Wichita. Total built: 160. Price: negotiated. Engine: two Continental O-470-M, 240 hp; gross weight: 4830 pounds; maximum speed: 232 mph; wingspan: 36 feet; service ceiling: 20,400 feet; single-engine: 7500 feet.

MODEL U-3B   ATC 3A10   1960

The air force's success with the U-3A, especially in the area of general operating and maintenance costs (USAF survey after one year in service with U-3A indicated direct operating costs were less than $12 per hour) coupled with the airplane's reliability record and popularity with pilots prompted the government to buy 36 airplanes in 1960. Designated U-3B (310E by Cessna), they were equivalent to the 1961 Model 310F and all were built at the Military Aircraft Division factory in west Wichita. Total built: 36. Price: negotiated. Engine: two Contiental IO-470-D, 260 hp; gross weight: 4830 pounds; maximum speed: 242 mph; wingspan: 36 feet; service ceiling: 21,300 feet; single-engine: 7700 feet.

▲ MODEL 318/T-37   NO ATC ISSUED   1954

First flown on October 12, 1954 by Cessna test pilot Bob Hagan, the Model 318 was designed to meet a United States Air Force requirement for a new trainer that would transition pilots from reciprocating-engine to jet-engine powered aircraft. Cessna won a contract to develop its XT-37 in April, 1953 and by 1956 three prototypes (USAF s/n 54-716 to 54-718) had logged over 1000 test flights. Eleven pre-production T-37A (USAF s/n 54-2729 to 54-2739) were built in 1954/55 and production of the first 270 airplanes was in full swing by 1957/58. First deliveries of the T-37 to the air force began in 1957 and the very first all-jet pilot class to use the "Tweety-Bird", as it was affectionately known. started their training in November, 1958 and by April, 1961 the USAF dropped all piston-powered primary training from the flight curriculum. The T-37A was followed by the improved T-37B with more powerful engines in 1959 (all "A" models were eventually converted to "B" status). As of 1986, the T-37 is still the air force's basic trainer. Total built: 1954-77: 1272. Engine: two Continental (license built) J-69, 1025 lb. static thrust each; gross weight: 6600 pounds; maximum speed: 370 knots (1/2 fuel load, military thrust rating at sea level); wingspan: 33 feet seven inches; service ceiling: 35,100 feet; single-engine: 20,100 feet (1/2 fuel load, military thrust). T-37B is illustrated. (Reference Appendix A, #30)

MODEL 318/A-37A/A-37B   ▶
NO ATC ISSUED   1968

The T-37 went to war as the A-37A and the improved A-37B that was developed in 1968. The A-37B attack aircraft featured improved fire control system, aerial refueling probe and General Electric J-85-17A engines (A-37A had 2400 lb. static thrust J-85) that were canted downward and outward, minimizing the affect of thrust changes on pitch. Ailerons were equipped with redundant control systems and boost tabs that assisted roll control with full external stores mounted. First production USAF/Cessna A-37B was delivered in May, 1968. Inflight photograph of A-37B illustrates two 100-gallon external fuel tanks on inboard pylons, BLU-23B napalm tank and 2.75-inch rocket tube on outboard hardpoints. Removeable refueling probe extends from nose with blast tube for the General Electric 7.6mm GAU-28/A Minigun to right of probe. A-37B were being assigned to Air National Guard units by 1970. Total built: A-37A (Model 318D): 39 (note: all 39 A-37A were converted to T-37B during production); A-37B (Model 318E): 577. Engine: two General Electric J-85-17A, 2850 lb. static thrust each; gross weight, attack configuration: 14,000 pounds (maximum external ordnance load: 5680 pounds); maximum speed: 456 mph; wingspan: 35.88 feet. Service ceiling: 41,765; single-engine: 25,000 feet. Last A-37B produced: 6-14-77.

Instrument panel for prototype A-37B. ▼

A-37B instrument panel. ▼

▲ MODEL 319A EXPERIMENTAL 1953
The U.S. Naval Research Laboratory and Cessna teamed up in 1953 to fly the Model 319A for advanced boundary layer control (BLC) experiments. Using a standard L-19A fuselage with new, modified wings that incorporated primary/secondary flaps, drooping ailerons and a new empennage, an electric generator provided power to special fans mounted in the wings. Air from the fans was directed over the wing/control surfaces and resulted in very low airspeeds for takeoff and landing. The only Model 319A built, c/n 608, is illustrated. Note special test pitot tube on left wing, anemometers on right wing, gust locks on control surfaces. (Gordon S. Williams photo via Mitch Mayborn/Bob Pickett)

▼ MODEL 320 SKYKNIGHT ATC 3A25 1962
Cessna's Model 320 Skyknight was based on the 1961 Model 310F but featured extra cabin windows and 260 hp turbocharged engines that maintained sea level horsepower up to 16,000 feet. One prototype (c/n 635) was built in 1960 which incorporated changes that transformed the 310F into the new 320: wing section around the nacelles strengthened to accept heavier nacelle structure; overwing exhaust augmentor tubes deleted and nacelle trailing edge faired into upper wing skin; two ram air wing leading edge intakes, (one outboard of the nacelle for cooling airflow to the turbocharger, one inboard of the nacelle feeding the turbocharger compressor). A stainless steel heat shroud/firewall separated the engines from the wing. The fuselage was 3 1/2 inches deeper from the forward cockpit to the tail, providing increased head and leg room for aft occupants and horizontal stabilizer incidence was decreased. Tip tanks held 102 gallons of fuel with 133 gallons optional. Five-outlet oxygen system (less cylinder) was standard equipment. Segmented louvers beneath cowlings housed manually-operated cowl flaps. Planned for introduction in the fall of 1961, Cessna introduced the Skyknight in May with initial deliveries beginning in August. Total built: 1962 model year: 110 (production began in spring, 1961 but were 1962 models). Price: $67,500. Engine: two Continental TSIO-470-B, 260 hp; gross weight: 4990 pounds; maximum speed: 265 mph (16,000 feet); wingspan: 36 feet; service ceiling: 27,200 feet; single-engine: 17,300 feet (at 4990 pounds). A 1962 320 Skyknight is illustrated.

▲ MODEL 320A/B/C SKYKNIGHT
ATC 3A25   1963-65

The Skyknight received several improvements during its second year of production, including: 210-pound gross weight increase, pointed, more streamlined tip tanks, restyled interior, open-view control wheels, redesigned main landing gear struts for improved shock absorption, improved rudder counterbalance. For 1964 320B, changes were: optional wing lockers held 120 pounds each, new flap indicator with printed airspeed limitations. The 1965 Skyknight C featured restyled control wheels, left landing light relocated to tip tank aft fairing (right light optional). Total built: 1963: 47; 1964: 62; 1965: 74 (includes 320C prototype c/n 658). Engine: two Continental TSIO-470-B, 260 hp; gross weight: 5200 pounds; maximum speed: 263 mph (16,000 feet, 320C); wingspan: 36 feet 11 inches; service ceiling: 28,100 feet; single-engine: 16,600 feet (320C). A 1963 320A Skyknight is illustrated.

MODEL 320D EXECUTIVE SKYKNIGHT   ◄
ATC 3A25   1966

The 1966 Skyknight featured new design engine cowlings with integral cooling louvers, reshaped aft cabin window. Three-blade McCauley propellers were optional equipment, offered for the first time on the 1966 Executive Skyknight. Minor interior/cabin refinement decreased sound levels and optional long-range fuel tank capacity increased to 143 gallons. 285 hp engines were standard. Total built: 130. Engine: two Continental TSIO-520-B, 285 hp; gross weight: 5200 pounds; maximum speed: 275 mph; wingspan: 36 feet 11 inches; service ceiling: 29,300 feet; single-engine: 18,500 feet (5200 pound gross weight).

▼ MODEL 320E/F EXECUTIVE SKYKNIGHT
ATC 3A25   1967-68

Cessna made significant changes to the Skyknight series for 1967/68. Major improvements were: 320E: 100-pound gross weight increase, redesigned motor permitted landing gear extension up to 160 mph, 28% greater shock strut travel on main gear, fuselage nose cap lengthened six inches to allow field installation of radar, larger cabin entry steps, one-piece windshield without center post, combustion heater/cabin air intake relocated to right side of fuselage nose, pilot's storm window, fuselage baggage door moved 21-inches aft permitting easier loading without moving fifth/six seat forward, larger Model 411-type ailerons and wing trailing edge for improved lateral control increased wing area to 179 square feet, 1968 320F had 320E's improvements and: circuit breaker panel canted upward for easier readability, electroluminescent panel lighting, new, larger baggage door, optional forward wing locker fuel tanks holding 20 gallons each. The Executive Skyknight was not offered after 1968 model year. All Model 320-series (1962-68) featured 28-volt electrical systems standard. Total built: 1967: 110; 1968: 45. Price: $85,500 (320F). Engine: two Continental TSIO-520-B, 285 hp; gross weight: 5300 pounds; maximum speed: 235 mph; wingspan: 36 feet 11 inches; service ceiling: 29,000 feet; single-engine: 18,800 feet. 1968 Model 320F Executive Skyknight illustrated.

▲ MODEL 321/OE-2   ATC 3A11   1955

Using Model 180 wings and modified empennage, Cessna built the Model 321 for the U.S. Marines in 1955. A more powerful engine was installed on an entirely new fuselage and the airplane was capable of flying farther and faster while carrying more load than the L-19/OE-1. The 321 had armor plate for the pilot and flak curtains, electrically-operated flaps, circuit breakers, red instrument lighting. Designated OE-2 by the Marines, the airplane was well received but no further orders were forthcoming and Cessna's hopes of the U.S. Army ordering a large quantity to replace the smaller L-19/OE-1 series did not materialize. Price may have been a major factor since the OE-2 cost much more than the standard L-19. Deliveries started in the summer of 1955 and were completed before the end of the year. Total built: 25. Engine: Continental TSO-470-2, 265 hp; gross weight: 2650 pounds; maximum speed: 180 mph; wingspan: 36 feet; service ceiling: 26,000 feet. Model 321 first flight: 8-19-54; pilot: R.L. Crawshaw

▼ MODEL 325   NO ATC ISSUED   1953

Based primarily on the Model 305 but with stronger main gear, large wheels/brakes, more powerful engine and two-blade constant-speed propeller, the rough and ready Model 325 was developed and conceived by Cessna as a potential aerial application airplane, specialized to handle the task. Two examples were constructed in 1953 as proof-of-concept ships, sent to the field where spray booms/tanks were installed. The Model 325 was not produced since there was no solid market for the airplane. Cessna announced cancellation of the 325 program on September 13, 1955. One Model 325, c/n 24000 served in Santiago, Veraguas, Republic of Panama in the mid-1960s with Servicio Aereo Cantu S.A. in ag operations. Total built: four (two in 1953, two in 1956); Engine: Continental O-470, 230 hp; wingspan: 36 feet. Airplane illustrated is actually a Model 305/prototype Model 325 with spray equipment installed. Note hopper tank located behind front seat, sealed aft windows, air-driven spray pump. Model 325 first flight pilot: R.L. Crawshaw

▼ MODEL 335   ATC 3A25   1980

Produced during the 1980 model year only, the Model 335 was certificated under the same ATC as the older 320 Skyknight series, and, sharing many airframe/engine systems with its pressurized counterpart the Model 340A, was intended to be an entry-level light twin replacing the aging but popular Model 310. The Model 335 also appealed to business pilots desiring to make the step up from over-the-wing cabin entry twins like the Piper Aztec and Beech Baron to a cabin-class ship with an airstair door. To make the 335 less expensive in the marketplace, Cessna deleted pressurization but retained a comfortable six-seat cabin and turbocharged engines. Air conditioning, writing tables, 40 and 63-gallon auxiliary fuel tanks were optional and the 335 II preferred options package was available. Total built: 65. Price: $209,950. Engine: two Continental TSIO-520-EB, 300 hp; gross weight: 5990 pounds; maximum speed: 230 knots (16,000 feet); wingspan: 38 feet 1.3 inches; service ceiling: 26,800 feet; single-engine: 11,500 feet.

1980 Model 335 instrument panel. ▼

▲ MODEL 377/327 EXPERIMENTAL 1965-68
Designed as a low-cost, high performance multi-engine airplane with center-line thrust, the 1965 proposed Model 377 incorporated a full cantilever wing very similar to the Model 210 Centurion combined with the twin-boom layout of the Model 337 Skymaster. Changed to Model 327 in 1967, one experimental prototype, c/n 663, N3769C was built, flying on December 4, 1967 with two 160 hp O-320 engines and McCauley 72-inch diameter constant-speed propellers, reaching 187 mph during initial tests. Over 38 hours of flight testing were completed before the Model 327 project was cancelled in 1968 but the airplane soldiered on as a Langley Research Center/Cessna noise reduction testbed for wind tunnel evaluation of ducted and free propellers. Total built: one. Engine: two Lycoming O-320, 160 hp; gross weight: 3500 pounds; maximum speed: 187 mph; wingspan: 35 feet six inches; single-engine service ceiling (flight test only, front engine): 6300 feet. Model 327 first flight: 12-4-67; pilot: G.M. Baker

▲ MODEL 336   ATC A2CE   1963-64
Designed as a new concept in lightweight, multi-engine airplanes, the Model 336 with its unique center-line thrust configuration first flew on February 28, 1961 flown by test pilot Bill Thompson. Designed under the direction of Donald Ahrens, the 336 seated six people under a semi-cantilever wing with two metal fuel tanks and the horizontal stabilizer/elevator/rudder were mounted on two elliptical booms projecting aft from cabin. Fixed, tri-cycle landing gear was selected for simplicity and cost reduction.

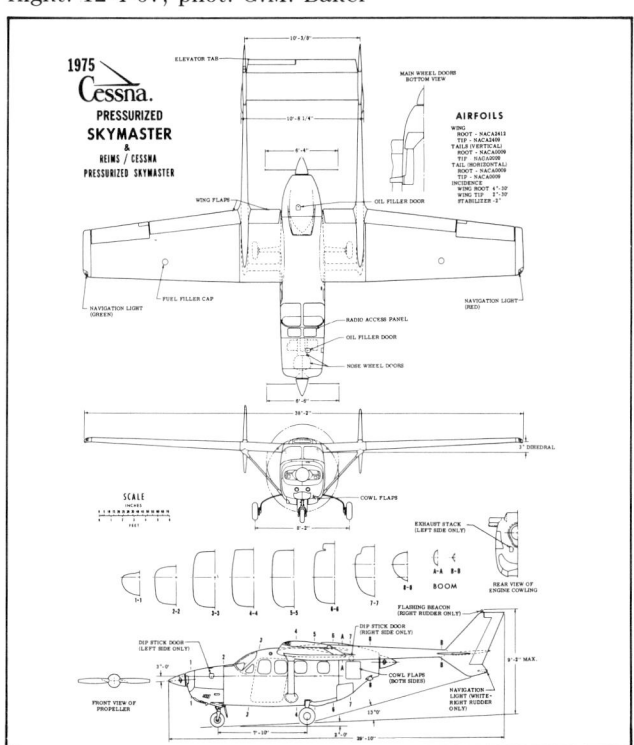

1967 Model 337B Super Skymaster instrument panel. ▲

After redesigning the cabin for more room, changing the rear engine cowl to decrease cabin noise level and improve aft engine cooling, certification was completed in May, 1962. The FAA issued a CLT rating restricted for center-line thrust only for the Model 336 and Cessna's Senior Vice President Del Roskam was the first pilot to receive approval. Total built: 1963-64: 197. Engine: two Continental IO-360-A, 210 hp; gross weight: 3900 pounds; maximum speed: 183 mph; wingspan: 38 feet; service ceiling: 19,000 feet; front engine only: 8200 feet; aft engine only: 9500 feet. Three Model 336 Skymasters illustrated are early 1963 production airplanes.

MODEL 337/T337 SUPER SKYMASTER
ATC A6CE   1970-72

Performance and comfort improvements on the 337 series continued into the seventies, starting with the 1970 Model 337E featuring new, capacitance-type fuel quantity system (readout in gallons), useful load increased 35 pounds, maximum gear extension speed increased to 160 mph, conical-cambered wingtips, gross weight increased 40 pounds, auxiliary fuel level alert annunciator (1970 was also the first year for Reims-produced Model F337 Skymaster). 1971 337F: padded glareshield and instrument subpanels/doorposts, fuel gauges readout in pounds/gallons, restyled interior, new, front engine access panel for spark plug servicing, improved fuel selector valve, tape-type wiring harness in control column. 1972 337F: cowl-mounted taxi/landing lights, padded control wheels, avionics audio panel/annunciators in glareshield, turbocharging option deleted. Total built: 1970: 100; 1971: 61; 1972: 53. Reims F337: 1970-72: 42. Price: $51,250 (1971). Engine: two Continental IO-360-C, 210 hp; TSIO-360-A, 210 hp (T337); gross weight: 4440 pounds (1970), 4630 pounds (1970 T337), 4630 pounds (1971 337/T337) maximum speed: 230 mph (1971 T337); wingspan: 38 feet two inches (1970 and after); service ceiling: 29,300 feet; front engine: 14,400 feet; aft engine: 17,200 feet (T337). A 1970 337E Super Skymaster is illustrated. Model T337G first flight pilot: P.R. Leckman.

MODEL 337   SUPER SKYMASTER
ATC A6CE   1965

In 1965 Cessna redesigned the 336 into a highly improved airplane called the 337 Super Skymaster. Most significant change was retractable landing gear system very similar in operation to the Model 210 installation. A hydraulic pump was driven by the front engine to provide fluid power. Other important improvements were a larger, fixed aft engine air scoop, wing angle of incidence changed two degrees 30 minutes for better forward visibility in cruise flight, vertical stabilizer ventral fins shortened by six inches to avoid damage caused by overrotation on takeoff and overflare on landing, elevator chord was increased four inches to augment pitch authority and the airplane sat four inches closer to the ground, making cabin entry/exit easier. Total built: 240 (including prototype c/n 656). Engine: two Continental IO-360-C and IO-360-D, 210 hp; gross weight: 4200 pounds; maximum speed: 200 mph (sea level); wingspan: 38 feet; service ceiling: 20,500 feet; front engine: 8200 feet; aft engine: 10,200 feet. Model 337 first flight: 3-30-64; pilot: R.B. Kemper

MODEL 337/T337 SUPER SKYMASTER
ATC A6CE   1966-69

Continued changes to the 337-series from 1966 to 1969 included: 1966 337A: rotary-type door latches, canted engine instruments. 1967 337B: 38-ampere alternators, improved brakes, singular cabin fresh air outlets, redesigned heater plenum/outlets for more heat, split-bus electrical system, turbocharging option offered for the first time. 1968 337C: metal-to-metal seat belts. 1969 337D: elevator chord reduced four inches, elevator up travel increased, electroluminescent instrument panel lighting, toggle switch cowl flap controls. A 1967 337B Super Skymaster is illustrated. Total built: 1966: 285; 1967: 230; 1968: 223; 1969: 215. Engine: two Continental IO-360-C and D (1966-67), IO-360-C (1968), 210 hp; TSIO-360-A and B (1967-68), TSIO-360-A (1969), 210 hp; gross weight: 4200 pounds (1966), 4300 pounds (1967), 4400 pounds (1968), 4500 pounds (1968 T337); maximum speed: 200 mph; wingspan: 38 feet; service ceiling: 20,000 feet; front engine: 7500 feet; aft engine: 9500 feet.

MODEL 337/T337 SUPER SKYMASTER
ATC A6CE 1973-80

Cessna refined its push-pull 337 series from 1973-80 with improvements that included: 1973 337G: aerodynamic cleanup with recontoured nose cap, low-drag front engine exhaust stack, flush wingtip lights, low-drag wing strut fairings, flush-mounted (left wing strut) pitot port, aileron gap seals; air-stair door replaced cabin/baggage doors, hydraulic powerpack in pedestal replaced engine-driven pump. 1974 337G: improved subpanel rocker switches, recessed parking brake control, hydraulic gear accumulator. 1975 337G: Skymaster II preferred options package offered for first time, redesigned auxiliary fuel system offered with 148 gallons useable. 1976 337G: Camber-Lift wing, redesigned instrument panel with more avionics capacity, boom fuel sump tank eliminated, wing fuel system revised. 1977 337G: avionics master power switch, new front propeller airfoil improved single-engine rate of climb 10%. 1978-80 337H/T337H: turbocharging option returned after six year absence, restyled control wheels, minor interior refinements. Reims Aviation in France was assigned worldwide manufacturing rights for the Skymaster series in May, 1980, including any future U.S. commercial/military sales as Cessna withdrew the Super Skymaster from U.S. production after 1867 337/T337 had been produced. Total built: 1973: 81; 1974: 48; 1975: 60; 1976: 74; 1977: 62; 1978: 57; 1979: 47; 1980: 30. Engine: two Continental IO-360-G, IO-360-GB (1980), 210 hp; TSIO-360-H (1978-79), TSIO-360-HB (1980), 210 hp; gross weight: 4630 pounds; maximum speed: 172 knots; wingspan: 38 feet two inches; service ceiling: 16,300 feet; front engine: 6900 feet; aft engine: 7100 feet. A 1975 337G Super Skymaster is illustrated.

MODEL P337 PRESSURIZED SKYMASTER
ATC A6CE 1973-80

Cessna's pressurized Model P337 introduced in 1973 featured 250 mph maximum speed, 3.35 psi cabin pressure differential, 225 hp turbocharged engines and 123 gallons of useable fuel. Other changes were: 365 pounds of baggage capacity, recontoured front cowling improved fuselage boundary layer airflow, new gear hydraulic powerpack replaced engine-driven pump. 1974 models had improved airstair door lift, gear accumulator, improved rocker switches while 1975 versions featured 148 gallons useable fuel standard, Skymaster II package optional. In 1975, full flap extension speed increased to 110 knots, 1/3 flaps to 165 knots, airspeed indicator in knots only. 1977 P337G had avionics master power switch, optional weather

1970 Model T337E Turbo Super Skymaster instrument panel.

radar for first time while 1978-80 P337 had only minor interior refinements. 1980 was the last production year for the P337 after 334 had been manufactured in the United States. Total built: 1973: 140; 1974: 40; 1975: 30; 1976: 30; 1977: 30; 1978: 25; 1979: 23; 1980: 15. Reims built 23 FP337 from 1973-80. Price: $78,500 (1973), $112,950 (1980). Engine: two Continental TSIO-360-C (1973-79), TSIO-360-CB (1980), 225 hp; gross weight: 4700 pounds; maximum speed: 212 knots (20,000 feet); wingspan: 38 feet two inches; maximum certified operating altitude; 20,000 feet. A 1977 Model P337G Pressurized Skymaster II is illustrated.

▲ MODEL M337 (O-2A/B)   ATC A6CE   1967-70

In 1967 the United States Air Force needed a Forward Air Control (FAC) airplane in Vietnam with twin-engine redundancy, good downward visibility and the capability to take punishment from small arms fire yet defend itself with small-caliber offensive weapons and rockets. They found what they needed in the Cessna Skymaster. Designated M337/MC337 for the O-2A and O-2B respectively, the O-2A mounted four underwing pylons for rockets and the 7.62 mm Minigun pack but the extra weight made a military O-2A much heavier than its civilian counterpart. Large, clear, acrylic observation windows were installed in the cabin door/right forward fuselage giving a good look at the ground. The O-2B used big speakers and a leaflet dispenser to fight the enemy as a psychological warfare ship in Southeast Asia and appeared very similar to commercial Skymasters. Advanced projects for the M337 included the O-2T with two Allison 250 turboprops that flew in 1967-68. A stretched, tandem-seat O-2TT with turboprops was built in mockup form only. Total built: O-2A: 479; O-2B: 31. O-2A 67-21295 (c/n M337-0001) is illustrated.

1977 Model P337 instrument panel. ▲

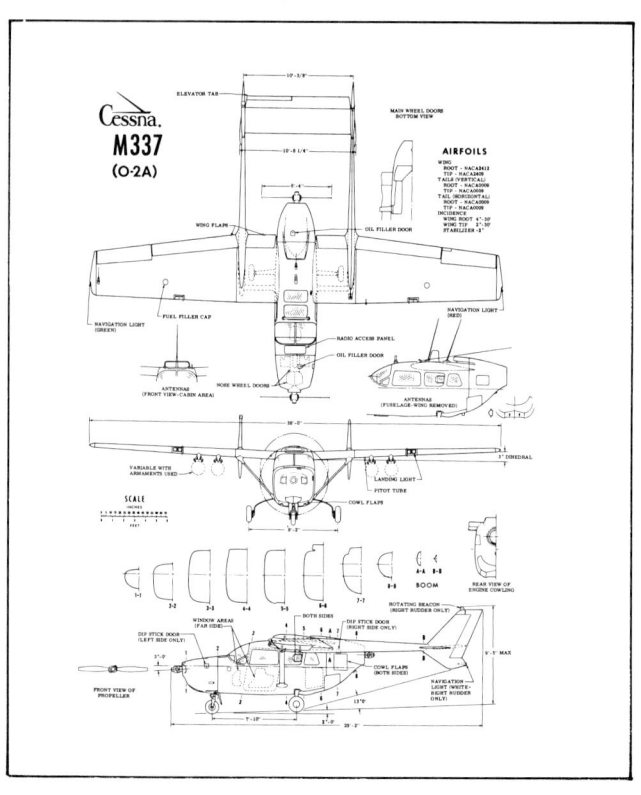

MODEL 340 ATC 3A25 1972-75

To expand their line of pressurized, multi-engine airplanes, Cessna built two prototypes (c/n 672 and c/n 673) in 1970 and then introduced the new Model 340 in 1972 equipped with 4.2 psi cabin pressure differential, two-piece airstair door, 100 gallons of fuel in tip tanks, capacitance-type fuel quantity system, electrically-operated landing gear, two-blade propellers standard (78-inch diameter three-blade units optional) and 285 hp turbocharged, fuel-injected engines. In 1974 the 340 II preferred options package was offered for the first time, a frameless pilot storm window was standard and Cessna-designed air conditioning system was available. 1975 340 had improved pressurization outflow/safety valves and optional surface de-ice equipment for first time, three-blade propellers were standard with 40 or 63-gallon auxiliary fuel tanks optional. Total built: 1972: 115; 1973: 110; 1974: 70; 1975: 55. Engine: two Continental TSIO-520-K, 285 hp; gross weight: 5975 pounds; maximum speed: 226 knots (16,000 feet); wingspan: 38 feet 1.1 inches; service ceiling: 26,500 feet; single-engine: 12,100 feet. A 1974 Model 340 is illustrated.

MODEL 340A ATC 3A25 1976-85

Higher horsepower engines, new cowlings, refined seats and interior furnishings were hallmarks of the improved Model 340A of 1976. Installation of 310 hp engines (same as used on the larger Model 414) increased maximum speed 17 mph and gross weight was increased 40 pounds. The 1977 340A featured improved airstair door operation, polyurethane paint and revised flap control to standardize the 340A with other Cessna twins. Only refinements made to the 1978 version were new control wheels with larger grip horns and introduction of the 340 III preferred options package with ARC 400-series avionics, 63-gallon auxiliary fuel tanks, variable pressurization control system standard. 1984 Model 340A TBO increased from 1400 to 1600 hours, variable rate pressurization system, dual flight controls

standard. By 1982 model year, 1283 Model 340/340A had been manufactured. Total built: 1976: 125; 1977: 175; 1978: 162; 1979: 201; 1980: 145; 1981: 80; 1982: 43; 1983: none; 1984: 16; 1985/86: no c/n assigned. Price: $210,450 (1977). Engine: two Continental TSIO-520-N, 310 hp (1976-78), TSIO-520-NB, 310 hp (1979); gross weight: 5990 pounds; maximum speed: 244 (20,000 feet); wingspan: 38 feet 1.3 inches; service ceiling: 29,800 feet; single-engine: 15,800 feet. 1977 Model 340 II illustrated.

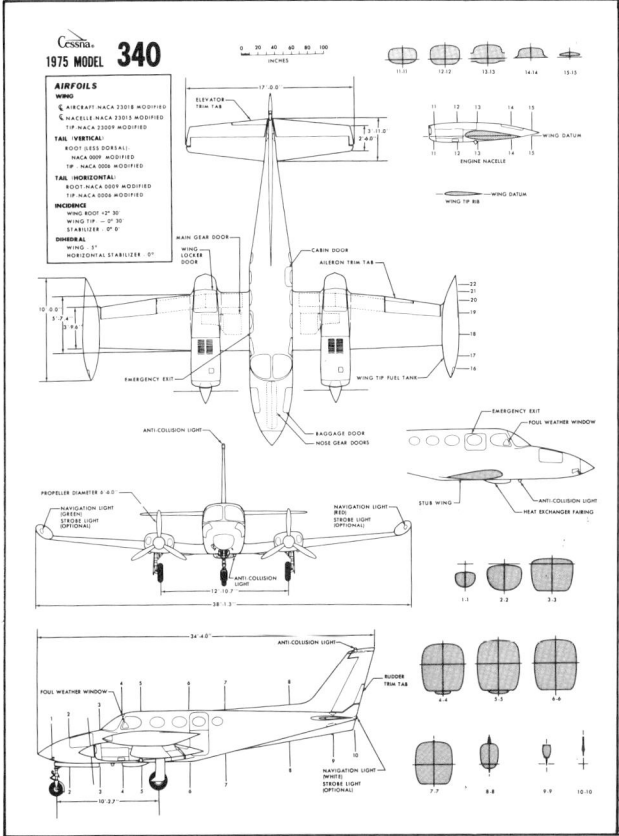

1974 Model 340 instrument panel. ▼

1980 Model 340A instrument panel. ▼

▲ MODEL 401   ATC A7CE   1967
Cessna's 400-series, new generation light twin-engine airplanes were introduced in the middle 1960s with the Model 401 being offered in 1967. Designed as a cabin-class twin above Model 310/320, the 401 featured new cabin volume and comfort with seating for six to eight occupants. Powered by 300 hp turbocharged, fuel-injected engines turning three-blade, constant-speed, full-feathering propellers, turbocharging gave the 401 sea level horsepower up to 16,000 feet, a combination toilet/passenger seat was optional, 100 gallons of useable fuel were carried in two wing tip tanks with 40-gallon wing or 20-gallon wing locker tanks available. Electrically-operated split-type flaps, gear and 930 pounds of baggage capacity were standard features. Total built: 1967: 92. Price: $96,500. Engine: two Continental TSIO-520-E, 300 hp; gross weight: 6300 pounds; maximum speed: 228 mph (sea level); wingspan: 39.86 feet; service ceiling: 26,180 feet; single-engine: 11,700 feet. A 1967 Model 401 is illustrated. Model 401 first flight: 8-26-65; pilot: R.L. Crawshaw

▼ MODEL 401A/401B   ATC A7CE   1968-72
Popularity and sales of the new Model 401 were good and Cessna improved its cabin twin in 1969 with turbocharger overboost valves, new flap pre-select control, optional alternator fail annunciators, 100-ampere alternators (50-ampere standard), quick-remove circuit breaker panel, restyled interior. The 1970 401B introduced a redesigned flight deck with easier to read instrumentation, flight instruments grouped in basic "T" arrangement, relocated engine instrument clusters, gray panel color, capacitance-type fuel quantity system with pounds/gallons readout. A cargo/airstair door was optional. For 1971-72 the 401B featured stainless steel turbocharger heat shields and bonded upper engine nacelle, three-green gear down annunciator lights were standard for the first time. Air conditioning and surface de-ice equipment was optional. The Model 401B was not offered after the 1972 model year. Total built: 1968: 91; 1969: 132; 1970: 49; 1971: 21; 1972: 21. As of 1972 model year, 406 Model 401/401A/401B had been built. Price: $109,950 (1970 401B). Engine: two Continental TSIO-520-E, 300 hp; gross weight: 6300 pounds; maximum speed: 228 mph (sea level); wingspan: 39.86 feet; service ceiling: 26,180 feet; single-engine: 11,700 feet. 1972 Model 401B is illustrated.

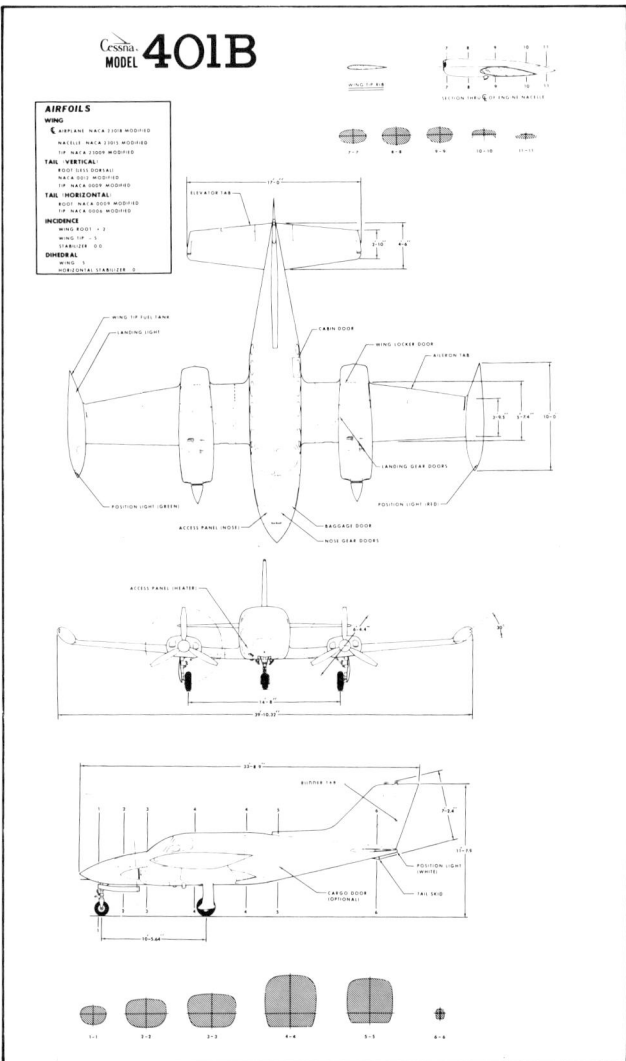

1969 Model 401A instrument panel.

MODEL 402/402A ATC A7CE 1967-68

A sharp increase in air taxi and cargo operations occurred in the late 1960s and Cessna responded with the Model 402 "Utilitwin", designed with 222.4 cubic foot interior that could be easily and quickly converted from passenger to cargo configuration. A two-piece airstair door was standard with a cargo/airstair door, 40 gallon wing tanks or 20 gallon wing locker tanks optional. A 1967 Model 402 is illustrated. Total built: 1967: 69; 1968: 70. Engine: two Continental TSIO-520-E, 300 hp; gross weight: 6300 pounds; maximum speed: 228 mph (sea level); wingspan: 39.86 feet; service ceiling: 26,180 feet; single-engine: 11,700 feet.

MODEL 402A/B ATC A7CE 1969-72

A new, stretched nose section was featured on the 1969 Model 402A, holding up to 600 pounds of baggage. Turbocharger overboost valves were standard equipment to prevent engine damage from excessively high manifold pressures. Wing, tail and propeller de-ice was optional as was the cockpit hatch-type door. In 1970 the Model 402B featured a capacitance-type fuel quantity system, easier-to-read instrumentation, revised system-status annunciator panel, improved engine cooling to decrease cylinder head temperatures. The 1972 402B "Businessliner" or "Utililiner" was available as either a passenger or cargo airplane, a second forward nose baggage door was offered as an option while three green gear down annunciator lights and bonded upper engine cowlings were standard. Total built: 1969: 129; 1970: 43; 1971: 22; 1972: 49. Price: $110,840 (1970). Engine: two Continental TSIO-520-E, 300 hp; gross weight: 6300 pounds; maximum speed: 228 mph; wingspan: 39.86 feet; service ceiling: 26,180 feet; single-engine: 11,320 feet. A 1969 Model 402A with optional pilot entry hatch and cargo door is illustrated.

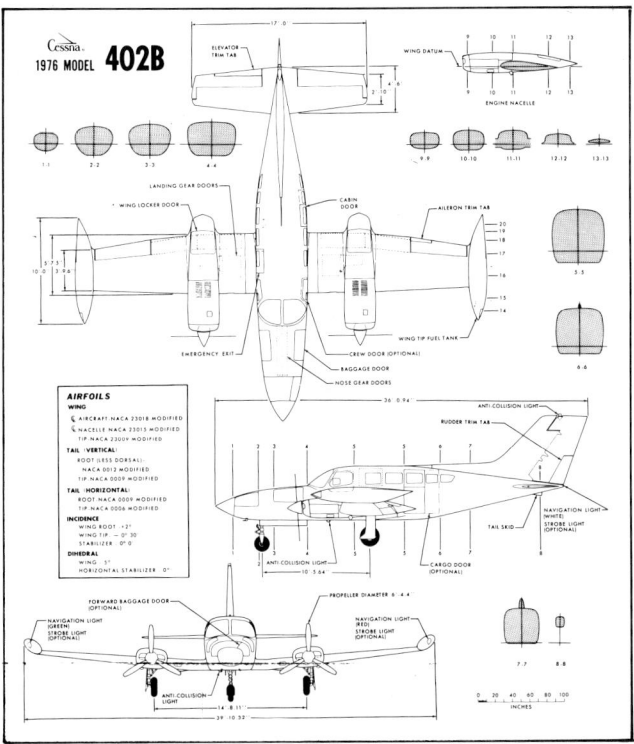

▲ MODEL 402B   ATC A7CE   1973-78
Major change for the six to eight-seat 1973 Model 402B was rectangular cabin windows with two extra panes, the cabin was 16 inches longer, instrument panel lowered 2 1/2 inches and canted back eight degrees for improved instrument reading and forward visibility. Improved turbocharger controls made cold weather operations easier and a toilet was optional for the first time. The 1975 402B had new design, quickly removeable cabin seats standard and the 1977 model was first to offer the 402B II package. 1977 402B featured polyurethane exterior paint, In 1978 only minor interior refinements, restyled control wheels were featured in the last year of 402B production. Total built: 1973: 155; 1974: 140; 1975: 135; 1976: 100; 1977: 50; 1978: 84. Engine: two Continental TSIO-520-E, 300 hp; gross weight: 6300 pounds; maximum speed: 229 knots (16,000 feet); wingspan: 39 feet 11 inches; service ceiling: 26,180 feet; single-engine: 11,320 feet. A 1978 Model 402B is illustrated.

▼ MODEL 402C   ATC A7CE   1979-85
Cessna incorporated some major changes into the 402C of 1979 including bonded wet wing with a capacity of 204 gallons giving a range of 1234 statute miles with IFR reserves, increased useful load of 2780 pounds and 325 hp engines that gave the 402C a single-engine climb rate of 301 feet per minute. Redesigned main landing gear doors, 1000-pound baggage capacity and the new wing increased propeller to fuselage clearance almost 5 1/2 inches. Both Businessliner and Utililiner versions were offered in 1979 and the new 402C Businessliner III preferred options package was offered with ARC 400-series avionics including Bendix RDR-160 weather radar. Total built: 1979: 125; 1980: 155; 1981: 128; 1982: 53; 1983: none; 1984: 6. As of 1982 model year, 1509 Model 402/402A/402B/402C had been built. Engine: two Continental TSIO-520-VB, 325 hp; gross weight: 6850 pounds; maximum speed: 231 knots (16,000 feet); wingspan: 44.12 feet; service ceiling: 26,900 feet; single-engine: 14,800 feet. A 1984 Model 402C is illustrated.

▲ **MODEL 404 TITAN   ATC A25CE   1977-81**
Cessna introduced the Model 404 Titan in 1977, featuring 375 hp geared, turbocharged, fuel-injected engines. With a cabin three feet longer than the 402C, the Titan was offered in three versions: Ambassador featuring a business interior, Courier with quick-change capability from people to cargo hauling and the Freighter, a heavy-duty cargo airplane capable of accepting "D"-size shipping containers with its optional, extra-wide loading doors. Technical innovations found on the new Titan included a bonded wet wing with a capacity of 340 gallons useable fuel, redesigned vertical stabilizer and horizontal stabilizer featured 12 degree dihedral for improved lateral stability and pitch control; hydraulically-operated, trailing-beam landing gear and large, Fowler-type wing flaps, new propeller airfoil section. In 1981 Cessna halted Titan production after a downturn in the commuter/cargo market that was aggravated by high interest rates. 397 Titans had been delivered by 1981. Total built: 1977: 136; 1978: 46; 1979: 60; 1980: 95; 1981: 59. Price: $263,950 (1977). Engine: two Continental GTSIO-520-M, 375 hp; gross weight: 8400 pounds; maximum speed: 232 knots (16,000 feet); wingspan: 46.33 feet; service ceiling: 26,000 feet; single-engine: 10,100 feet. A 1977 Model 404 Titan is illustrated.

MODEL F406   ATC A25CE (AMENDED)   1983 ➤
Developed by Cessna and its French affiliate Reims Aviation with the cooperation of the French Government, the twin turboprop Model F406 was designed at Wichita under the direction of Chuck Braden, project engineer, with all prototypes being fabricated and built in France. The Caravan II utilizes Model 404 Titan fuselage with Conquest I nose section, the vertical stabilizer uses many Conquest II component parts and the cruciform horizontal stabilizer was designed specifically for the F406. The Caravan II shares its center wing sections with the Conquest II while the nacelle/cowling assemblies and engine installation are based on the Model 425 Corsair. First flown on September 22, 1983 at Reims, France, maximum payload is 3,539 pounds with a useful load of 4,474 pounds. Up to 12 seats can be installed in the cabin or the interior can be used to haul bulk freight loads. Standard avionics package features Sperry 400-series equipment and 1000A autopilot. Price: $1,095,000 (1983). Engine: two Pratt & Whitney of Canada PT6A-112, 500 shp (flat-rated); gross weight, 9360 pounds; maximum speed: 256 ktas (mid-cruise weight); wingspan: 49.5 feet; service ceiling: 31,000 feet; single-engine: 16,000 feet. Note: Model 406 received French certification under Certificat de Navigabilite' de Type #175. U.S. certification is under amended Model 404 ATC A25CE. F406 c/n F406-0003 illustrated at top of photo, F406-0006 in center is second airplane for French Customs service with F406-0005 at bottom. Photograph courtesy Reims Aviation (Jean Varga) via Bob Pickett.

▲ MODEL 411   ATC A7CE   1965-66

Cessna's first twin-engine airplane over 6000 pounds gross weight, the unpressurized Model 411 was an all-new development designed to compete with the Beechcraft Queen Air and the Aero Commander 680. The 411 was also the first of Cessna's new 400-series family of twins. With six to eight seats in a wide-oval cabin entered through a two-piece airstair door, the 411 featured 340 hp geared, turbocharged, fuel-injected engines, 100 gallon fuel capacity in wing tip tanks and 35 gallons in outer wing tanks standard (13 gallon wing locker tanks optional), forged aluminum alloy main/nose gear struts, metal-to-metal bonded gear doors and baggage door, electrically-operated gear/flap systems. A wide CG range from 8% to 26% MAC combined with 700 pounds of baggage capacity offered increased loading flexibility, a 28-volt electrical system using 50 ampere alternators and a 45,000 BTU combustion heater, three-blade, constant-speed, full-feathering propellers were standard. Total built: 1965: 63; 1966: 63. Price: $108,950 initially, guaranteed not to exceed $120,000 in 1965 model year. Engine: two Continental GTSIO-520-C, 340 hp; gross weight: 6500 pounds; maximum speed: 268 mph (16,000 feet); wingspan: 39.86 feet; service ceiling: 26,000 feet; single-engine: 13,200 feet. 1965 Model 411 prototype is illustrated.

▼ MODEL 411A   ATC A7CE   1967-68

Improvements to the basic Model 411 created the 411A in 1967 model year with 200 changes, among the most salient being increased baggage capacity, revised nose section with two baggage doors (one on each side), insulated ductwork improved cabin heating, refined interior layout, restyled control wheels, white instrument lighting, 90-inch diameter propellers (88-inch on 411), dual, automatically rendundant vacuum system, seventh seat option, upper nose section access panel for avionics servicing. A twin cargo door, 26-gallon auxiliary wing locker fuel tanks, AVQ-45 weather radar (offered for first time) were optional. After 1968 the Model 411A was replaced by the Model 401/402 series. Total built: 1967: 12; 1968: 13. Price: $113,950. Engine: two Continental GTSIO-520-C, 340 hp; gross weight: 6500 pounds; maximum speed: 232 mph (sea level); wingspan: 39.86 feet; service ceiling: 26,000 feet; single-engine: 13,000 feet. 1967 Model 411A is illustrated.

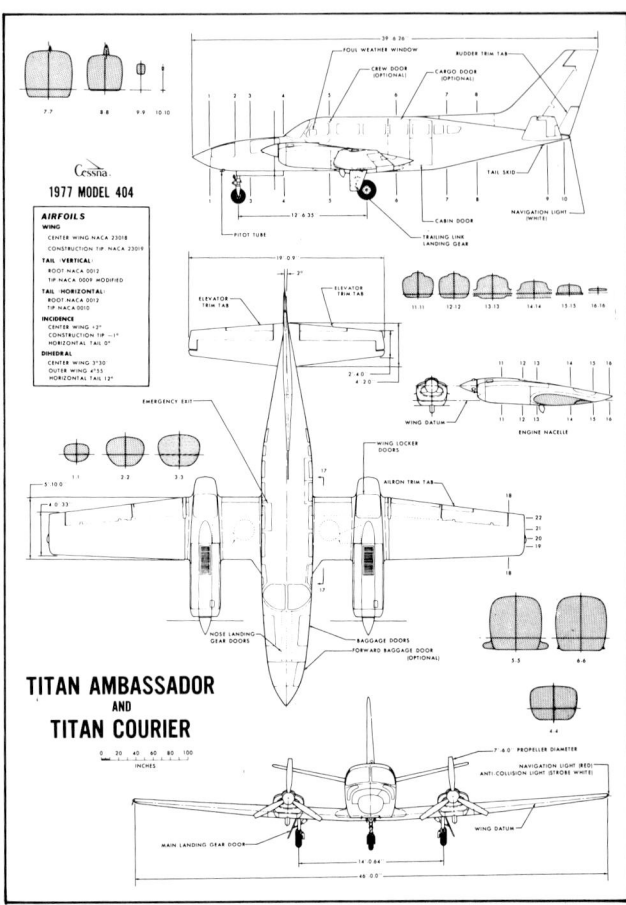

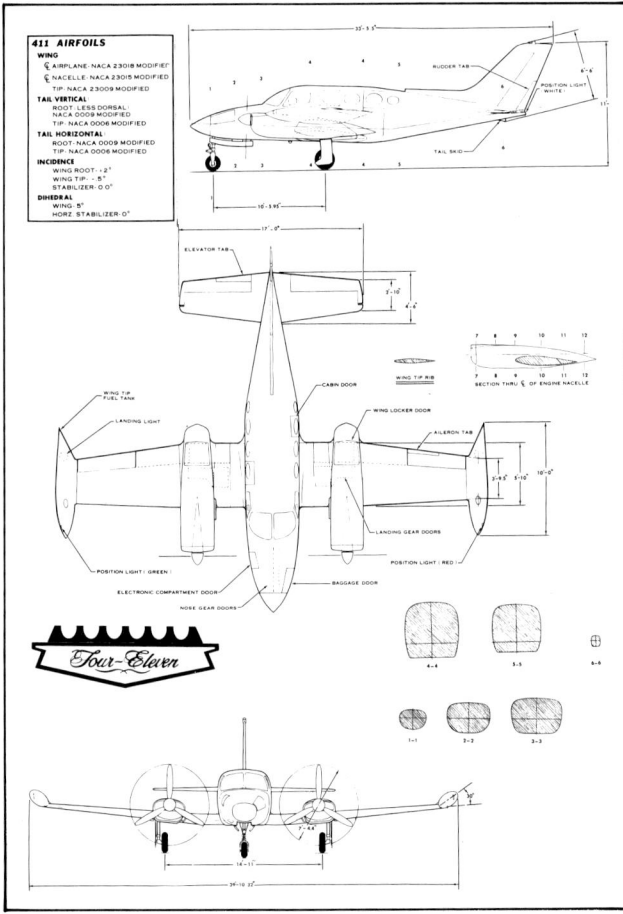

MODEL 414 ATC A7CE 1970-72

Cessna's third pressurized airplane, the 1970 Model 414 featured a 4.2 psi cabin differential, six or seven seats, maintained an 8000 foot cabin altitude at an airplane altitude of 20,000 feet, had a maximum range (no reserves) of 1432 sm with optional fuel tanks at 25,000 feet/225 mph, 100 gallon standard fuel capacity in wing tip tanks, 930 pounds of baggage, radiant heat circulation for cabin heating (augmented on the ground or in flight by a 45,000 BTU combustion heater), three-blade, constant-speed, full-feathering propellers and a 28-volt electrical system with 50-ampere alternators standard. Complete anti/de-ice equipment was optional. The Model 414 also featured the enlarged vertical stabilizer/dorsal fairing of the 401/402 series. 1972 changes included three green gear down annunciator lights, gear warning horn sounded when flaps were beyond 15 degrees/throttles retarded. Total built: 1970: 96; 1971: 25; 1972: 30. Price: $137,950 (1970). Engine: two Continental TSIO-520-J, 310 hp; gross weight: 6350 pounds; maximum speed: 272 mph (20,000 feet); wingspan: 39.86 feet; service ceiling: 30,100 feet; single-engine: 11,350 feet. A 1970 Model 414 is illustrated.

MODEL 414 ATC A7CE 1973-77

The 1973 Model 414 added an extra cabin window on each side, larger rear cabin area and new interior styling. Baggage capacity increased to 1090 pounds, instrument panel was lowered 2 1/2 inches to improve pilot's forward visibility, stainless steel turbocharger heat shields were incorporated and a new 63 gallon auxiliary fuel system was offered for the first time that, combined with the optional 40 gallon wing locker tanks brought maximum fuel capacity to 203 gallons. Electric windshield heat, automatically controlled, was also available. In 1976 Cessna introduced the Model 414 II preferred options package that included 400-series avionics, 63 gallon auxiliary fuel system and a

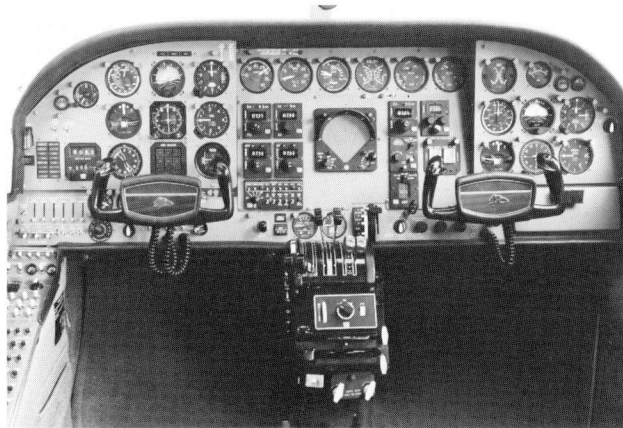

1972 Model 414 instrument panel.

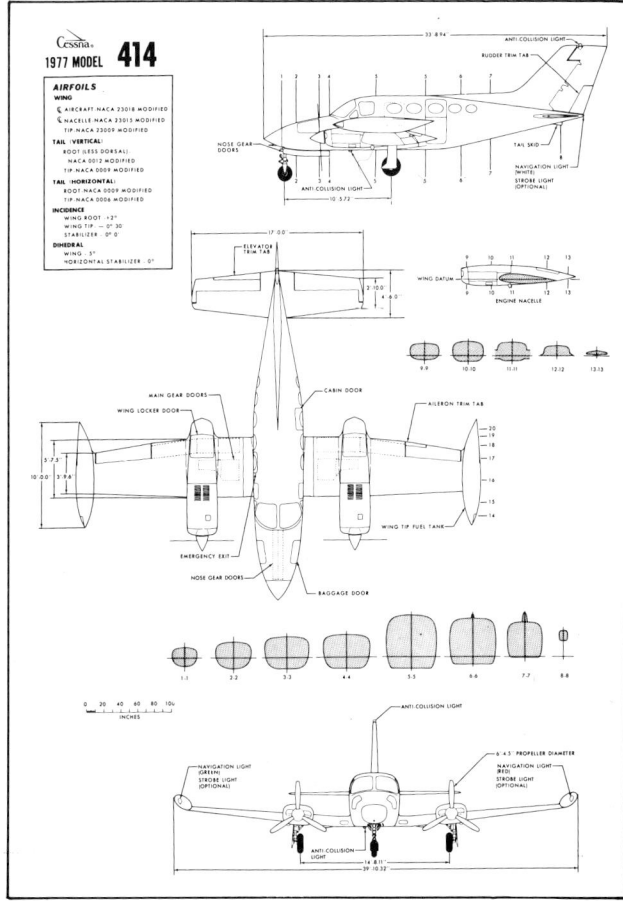

variable rate pressurization control system was standard. Changes for 1977 were a stronger tailcone, polyurethane exterior paint, new avionics circuit breaker panel on right cockpit side, hydraulic snubber unit on lower airstair door. After 1977 model year the 414 was superceded by the 414A Chancellor. Total built: 1973: 87; 1974: 100; 1975: 55; 1976: 55; 1977: 65. Price: $217,190 (1977). Engine: two Continental TSIO-520-J, 310 hp (1973-75), TSIO-520-N, 310 hp (1976-77); gross weight: 6350 pounds; maximum speed: 239 knots (20,000 feet); wingspan: 39 feet 11 inches: service ceiling: 30,100 feet; single-engine: 11,350 feet. 1975 Model 414 is illustrated.

▼ MODEL 414A CHANCELLOR   ATC A7CE   1978-85
A major redesign of the Model 414 resulted in the 414A Chancellor of 1978. Bonded, wet wing had a 44 foot span and 30 square feet more area, held 213.4 gallons of fuel standard. A higher vertical stabilizer was installed and a new, lengthened nose section with baggage door on each side was standard. Gross weight increased by 400 pounds and improved pressurization system featured 5.0 psi differential permitting 8500 foot cabin altitude at 24,000 feet. Hydraulic landing gear system replaced electric gear operation. The engines, housed in new cowlings, and the nacelles canted upward two degrees. In 1979, baggage capacity increased to 1500 pounds and the Chancellor III package with 1000-series ARC avionics, 100-ampere alternators and variable rate pressurization control system was available for first time. In 1984, engine TBO was increased from 1400 to 1600 hours, variable rate pressurization system, eight seats were standard. Total built: 1978: 121; 1979: 140; 1980: 135; 1981: 80; 1982: 58; 1983: none; 1984: 5. As of 1982 model year, 1049 414/414A Chancellor had been built. Engine: two Continental TSIO-520-N, 310 hp (1978), TSIO-520-NB, 310 hp (1979-85); gross weight: 6750 pounds; maximum speed: 235 knots (20,000 feet); wingspan: 44.12 feet; service ceiling: 30,800 feet; single-engine: 19,850 feet.

▲ MODEL 421   ATC A7CE   1968

Cessna's second pressurized airplane (first pressurized airplane was the 1956 Model 620) the Model 421 was developed in 1965-66 with c/n 657 as the prototype. Seating four to six in a wide-oval cabin entered through a two-piece airstair door, the 421 featured 4.2 psi cabin differential that permitted an 8000-foot cabin at an airplane altitude of 20,000 feet, with the capability to retain maximum differential down to 60% power on either engine. The standard pressurization system did not begin pressurizing the cabin until the airplane reached 8000 feet, then the cabin would pressurize until at 20,000 feet airplane altitude the cabin was at 8000 feet. A fully automatic, variable control system was optional. A 28-volt electrical system and 50 ampere alternators were standard with 100 ampere alternators optional. Complete oxygen system was also standard. Total built: 1968: 200. Price: $160,000. Engine: two Continental GTSIO-520-D, 375 hp; gross weight: 6800 pounds; maximum speed: 276 mph (16,000 feet); wingspan: 39.86 feet. service ceiling: 26,000 feet. A 1968 Model 421 is illustrated. Model 421 first flight: 10-14-65.

▼ MODEL 421A   ATC A7CE   1969

To make the popular Model 421 even better, Cessna improved its top-of-the-line twin in 1969 by introducing the Model 421A. Useful load increased 25 pounds, cruise speed was 261 mph at 22,500 feet and gross weight was 40 pounds more than its predecessor. Other changes were: new preselect flap control and indicator, revised headliner and window curtains, alternator fail annunciator lights, turbocharger overboost valves for pressure relief, improved seals on wing locker compartments. The 421A was built in 1969, being superseded by the 1970 pressurized 421B Golden Eagle. Total built: 158. Price: $172,500. Engine: two

Continental GTSIO-520-D, 375 hp; gross weight: 6840 pounds; maximum speed: 276 mph (16,000 feet); wingspan: 39.86 feet; service ceiling: 26,000 feet. The 1969 Model 421A prototype is illustrated.

1972 Model 421B Golden Eagle instrument panel. ▲

1977 Model 421C Golden Eagle instrument panel. ▲

▲ MODEL 421B   ATC A7CE   1970-75

1970 was the first year for a new kind of Model 421...the 421B Golden Eagle. A new nose section extended length 2.3 feet and featured a baggage door on each side for easy access to the 36 cubic foot compartment that held 600 pounds. Wingspan increased 2 feet, gross weight increased a hefty 410 pounds while useful load rose to 2890 pounds. The Golden Eagle could transport six people and their baggage at 260 mph over 1000 statute miles with 45 minutes reserve fuel thanks to its 170-gallon standard tanks with 248 gallons optional. Heavy-duty landing gear, wheels and brakes handled the higher gross weight and a capacitance-type fuel quantity system was used for the first time. 1973 421B had 5.0 psi differential, 10.4 cubic feet more cabin volume, 24% increase in viewing area from two extra cabin windows, 16-inch longer cabin, instrument panel lowered 2 1/2 inches/canted back eight degrees improving pilot's forward visibility. Ice protection equipment/air conditioning was optional.

An Executive Commuter version was available with 10 seats standard. In 1975 the 1000th Model 421 was delivered. Total built: 1970: 50; 1971: 46; 1972: 75; 1973: 186; 1974: 165; 1975: 170. Price: $187,500 (1970). Engine: two Continental GTSIO-520-H, 375 hp; gross weight: 7250 pounds; maximum speed: 237 mph (sea level); wingspan: 41.86 feet; service ceiling: 31,100 feet; single-engine: 13,000 feet. A 1975 Model 421B Golden Eagle is illustrated.

▼ 1968 Model 421 instrument panel with RCA AVQ-45 weather radar.

▲ MODEL 421C GOLDEN EAGLE   ATC A7CE   1976-85

The 1976 Golden Eagle featured a laminar flow, bonded wet wing that increased standard fuel capacity to 206 gallons with a 262-gallon system optional. Polyurethane exterior paint became standard in 1976 along with hydraulic landing gear that could be lowered at 175 mph, stronger tailcone, hydraulic snubber on lower airstair door, improved turbocharger intercoolers, large flange, wide-chord propeller blades; 10-inch higher vertical stabilizer and rudder, 2949-pound useful load. Ice protection equipment on wings, tail and propellers certified under FAR Part 25, Appendix C when installed. Golden Eagle II package offered for the first time in 1976 with 1000-series ARC avionics while 1978 421C offered the Golden Eagle III package that included as standard equipment a variable pressurization control system, air conditioning, 100 ampere alternators. The 1980 421C had new trailing-beam main landing gear with bonded doors, engine time between overhaul (TBO) prorated up to 1600 hours and underseat storage drawers in the cabin. 1984 421C had increased zero fuel weight from 6733 to 7000 pounds, rounded wing tip replaced with square tip design, variable rate pressurization system was included as standard. Total built: 1976: 171; 1977: 150; 1978: 125; 1979: 115; 1980: 110; 1981: 115; 1982: 57; 1983: none; 1984: 12; 1985: 6; 1986: no c/n assigned. As of 1982 model year, 1894 Model 421-series had been built. Price: $291,750 (1976 Golden Eagle), $338,150 (Golden Eagle II). Engine: two Continental GTSIO-520-L, 375 hp (1976-80), GTSIO-520-N, 375 hp (1981); gross weight: 7450 pounds; maximum speed: 258 knots (20,000 feet); wingspan: 41.12 feet; service ceiling: 30,200 feet; single-engine: 14,900 feet. A 1977 Model 421C Golden Eagle is illustrated.

▲ MODEL 425 CORSAIR   ATC A7CE   1980-83

Introduced in 1977-78, the Corsair was basically a Model 421C Golden Eagle airframe with additional three feet of wing span, stronger wing center section and a horizontal stabilizer with 12 degree dihedral. The Model 425 mounted two dependable Pratt & Whitney of Canada PT6A-112 reverse flow, free turbine turboprop engines flat-rated to 450 shp turning three-blade, constant-speed, full-feathering, reversible propellers. Hydraulically-operated, electrically-controlled gear system used trailing-beam design, dual engine-driven pumps for redundancy and 2000 psi nitrogen bottle for alternate extension. Standard fuel capacity was 366 gallons, a 5 psi differential permitted cabin altitude of 10,000 feet at an airplane altitude of 26,500 feet using variable rate controller. Up to 3405 pounds of useful load capacity, propeller, engine inertial separators (ice vanes) and pitot heat ice protection was standard with wing/tail de-ice boots optional. In 1983 Cessna changed the name to "Conquest I", starting with c/n 4250177. Total built (by calendar year): 1980: 42; 1981: 73; 1982: 60. Price: $825,000 (1980), $1,125,000 in 1984 model year for Model 425 Conquest I. Engine: two Pratt & Whitney of Canada, Ltd. PT6A-112, 450 shp (flat-rated); gross weight: 8200 pounds (1980-82), 8600 pounds (1983); maximum speed: 264 KIAS (18,700 feet); wingspan: 44.12 feet; service ceiling: 34,000 feet; single-engine: 19,000 feet. A 1980 Model 425 Corsair is illustrated. Model 425 first flight: 9-13-78; pilot: Rick Trissell.

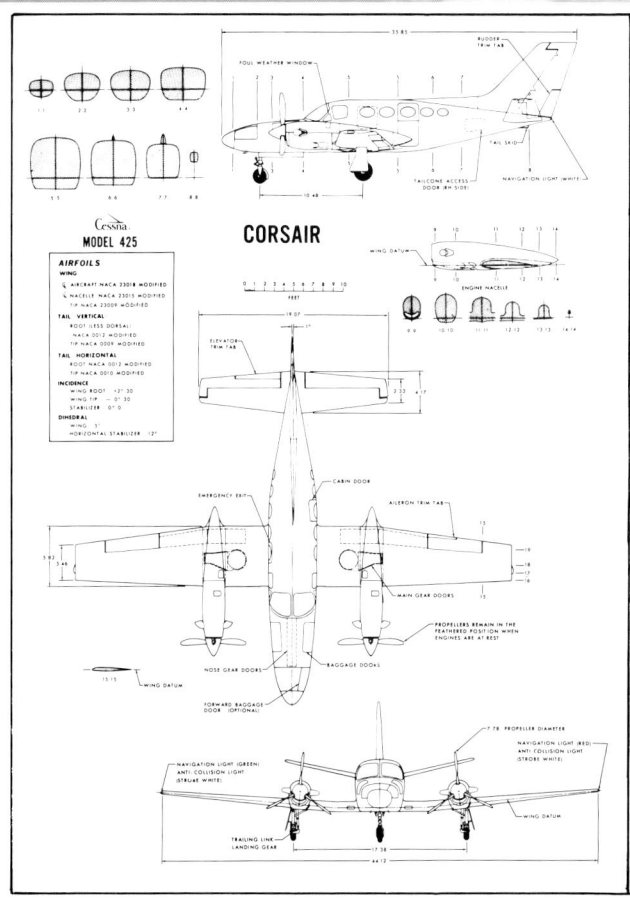

MODEL 441 CONQUEST ATC A28CE 1978-85

The Model 441 Conquest started life on paper as the Model 431 in 1972 with 435 hp Continental GTSIO-520-X engines/three-blade propellers but by 1975 had evolved into the turboprop Model 441, making its first flight on August 26, 1975. After 16 months of developmental testing and refinement on the prototype (c/n 679), the first production Model 441 propjet took to the air on January 10, 1977. Power for the eight to 10 seat pressurized, cabin-class Conquest came from two Garrett AiResearch TPE 331 fixed-shaft, turboprop engines that were flat-rated to 635 shp. A total of 468 gallons of fuel were carried in the bonded, wet wing that originally featured an aspect ratio of 8.7 and a span of 46.4 feet that was increased to 9.5 and 49.33 feet on early production airplanes. Pressure differential of 6.3 psid allowed a cabin altitude of 10,000 feet at an airplane altitude of 33,000 feet where the 441 cruised at 320 mph. Hydraulically-operated, electrically-controlled landing gear system and large, slotted Fowler-type flaps were standard, with two engine-driven hydraulic pumps for redundancy. 1984 models had lighter weight McCauley propellers (23 pounds lighter) replacing Hartzell units after constructor number 195. In 1983 Cessna renamed the Model 441 "Conquest II" (the Model 425 Corsair became Conquest I). Total built (by calendar year): 1978: 96; 1979: 78; 1980: 30; 1981: 49; 1982: 59 (including c/n 698, 1983 prototype). As of the 1982 model year, 313 Conquests had been built. Price: $1,795,000 (1983). Engine: two Garrett AiResearch TPE 331-8-401S, fixed-shaft, turboprop engine, 635.5 shp (flat-rated); gross weight; 9850 pounds; maximum speed: 293 knots (24,000 feet, 8350 pounds cruise weight); wingspan: 49.33 feet; service ceiling: 35,000 feet; single-engine: 21,380 feet. A 1978 Model 441 Conquest is illustrated.

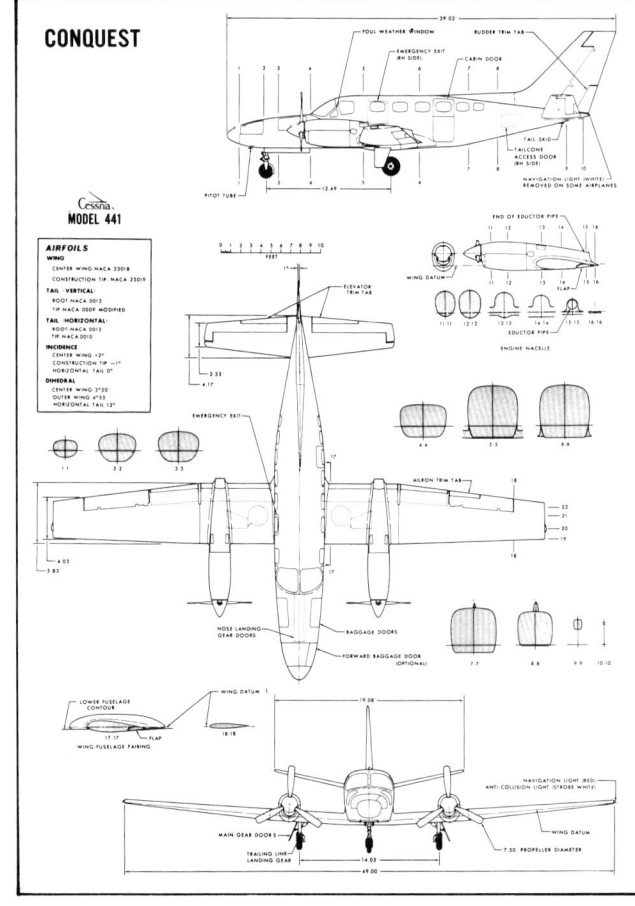

▲ MODEL 500 CITATION   ATC A22CE   1968

After a 10-year study of the executive jet market, Cessna announced its new Fanjet 500 in October, 1968, powered by the equally new Pratt & Whitney JT15D-1 turbofan engine. The name was officially changed to "Citation" on September 5, 1969 and the first prototype (N500CC) flew for the first time on September 15th, with pilots Milt Sills and J.L. Lesueur at the controls. Although outwardly similar to the Fanjet 500 mockup of 1968, the Citation featured a longer fuselage, higher vertical stabilizer, lowered horizontal stabilizer with 9 degree dihedral and relocated engine nacelles. The airplane was certified under FAR Part 25 (transport category) and required a type rating (turbofan engines). The Citation's 564 gallon fuel capacity gave it a respectable 910 sm range with six passengers and crew. Hydraulic landing gear, 28-volt electrical system, engine bleed air heating and cooling were standard. A 7.6 psi differential pressurization system permitted a sea level cabin up to 18,500 feet and complete ice protection equipment allowed full IFR operations. Engine thrust reversers (hydraulically-operated) were optional equipment. Total built (based on delivery to Cessna's Jet Marketing Division): 1971: 7; 1972: 51; 1973: 80; 1974: 84; 1975: 76; 1976: 48; 1977: 4. As of 1977 model year, 352 Citations had been built. Price: $695,000 (1972). Engine: two United Aircraft of Canada, Pratt & Whitney JT15D-1 turbofan engines, 2200 lbs. static thrust; maximum takeoff weight: 11,500 pounds, maximum landing weight: 11,300 pounds; maximum speed: Vmo: 287 KCAS; Mmo: 0.70 Mach; wingspan: 43 feet 11 inches; maximum operating altitude: 41,000 feet (c/n 214); 35,000 feet (c/n 1-213); single-engine service ceiling: 17,000 feet.

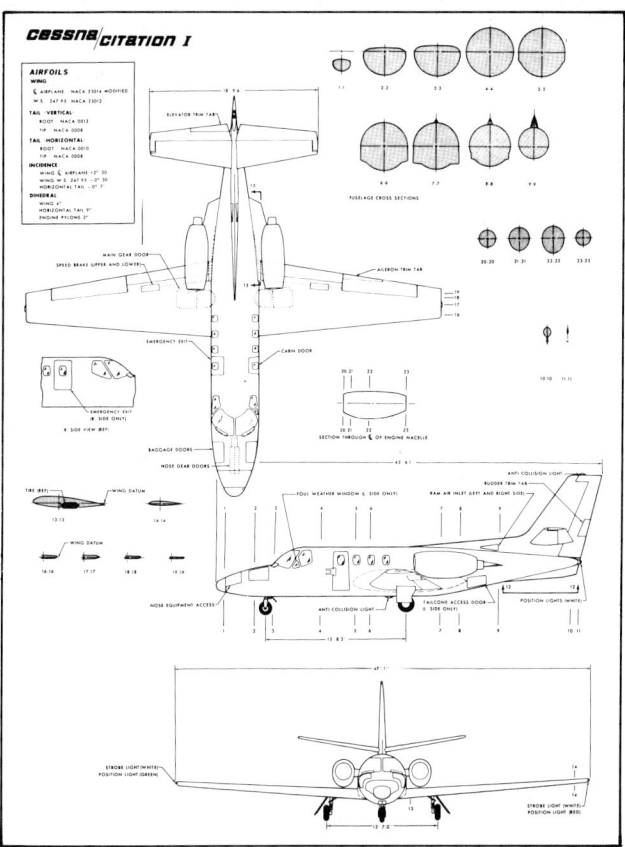

MODEL 500/501   ATC A22CE   ▶
(500)/ATC A27CE (501)   1977

Major improvements to the basic Citation created the Citation I and Citation I/SP. Wing span increased from 43 feet 11 inches to 47 feet 1 inch, improved JT15D-1A engines and a 1000-pound gross takeoff weight increase. Pressurization differential increased to 8.5 psid allowing an 8000-foot cabin at an airplane altitude of 41,000 feet, where the Citation I could fly six passengers and crew 1535 statute miles with 45 minute fuel reserves. In 1977 the Cessna Citation I/SP became the world's first business jet to receive approval for single-pilot operations and was issued a separate Approved Type Certificate (A27CE). Total built (combined Model 500/Model 501 based on delivery to Cessna's Jet Marketing Division): 1977-82: 315. Price:

$945,000 (1977). Engine: two Pratt & Whitney of Canada JT15D-1A, 2200 lbs. static thrust; maximum takeoff weight: 12,850 pounds (Citation I), maximum landing weight: 11,350 pounds; maximum speed: Vmo: 275 KCAS, Mmo: 0.70 Mach. Wingspan: 47 feet 1 inch; maximum operating altitude: 41,000 feet; single-engine service ceiling: 21,000 feet. First Citation I was c/n 350.

▲ MODEL 550/551   ATC A22CE   1978

By 1978 the Citation series had become the best-selling business jets in history. First flight of the improved Citation II was January 31, 1977 with Bob Leonard and Ellis Brady piloting the prototype airplane (N550CC). Redesigned wing with an aspect ratio of 8.3 and 150 additional gallons of fuel coupled with a 42-inch fuselage stretch and uprated JT15D-4 turbofans giving 14% more takeoff thrust were major improvements. The Citation II/SP model is restricted to a gross takeoff weight of 12,500 pounds (even if two crewmembers are on board), resulting in an 800-pound loss of useful load compared to the Citation II (note: a 1984 FAA ruling permits single-pilot operation of the II/SP at maximum 13,300-pound gross takeoff weight, but only if FAA-mandated pilot/equipment requirements are satisfied). Total built (based on delivery to Cessna's Jet Marketing Division): 1978: 34; 1979: 112. Price: $2,420,000 (1986): Engine: two Pratt & Whitney of Canada JT15D-4, 2500 lbs. static thrust; maximum takeoff weight: 13,300 pounds (12,500 pounds - II/SP); maximum speed: Vmo: 275 KCAS; Mmo: 0.70 Mach; wingspan: 51 feet 8 inches; maximum operating altitude: 43,000 feet; single-engine service ceiling: 26,500 feet. (Reference Appendix A, #31)

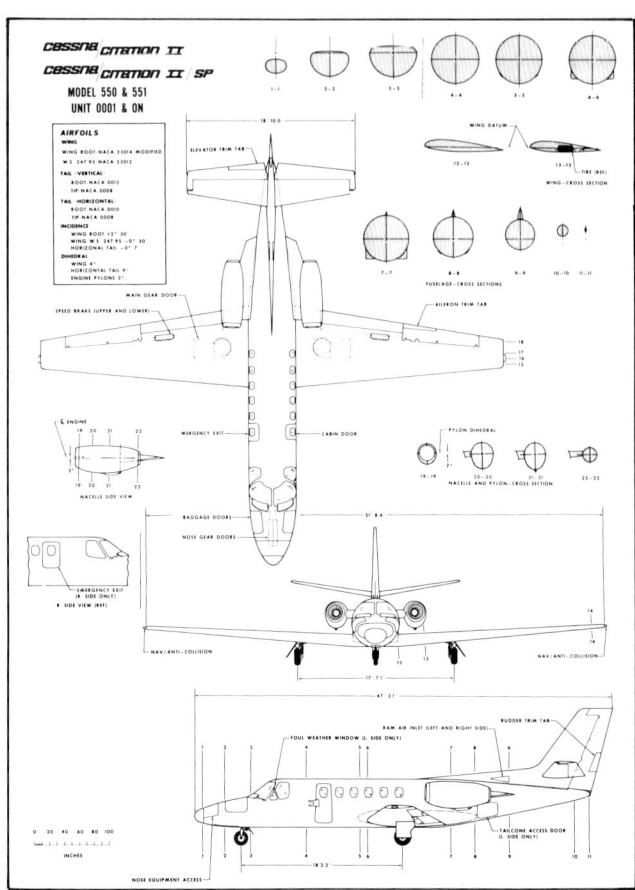

▼ MODEL S550/551 (S/II AND S/II SP)
   ATC A22CE   1984

Continuing to improve the Citation II concept, Cessna introduced the S/II and S/II SP in July, 1984. Supercritical wing technology created a different wing design with cuffs on the leading edge, revised airfoil cross-section to reduce drag at high cruise speeds, Fowler flaps were extended inboard, graphite ailerons with dual-geared trim tabs, gap seals for ailerons/flaps, recontoured wing/fuselage fairing and nacelles. Hydraulically-operated, electrically-controlled wing speed brakes employed on previous Citations were retained. TKS ethylene glycol wing/tail de-ice was standard, along with a 13% increase in fuel capacity to 862 gallons (5,820 lbs.) giving an 1800 nm range while cruising 403 KCAS (464 mph) at 35,000 feet. 8.8 psi differential permits an 8000-foot cabin at 43,000 feet. Target-type, hydraulically-controlled thrust reversers optional. Single-pilot approval of Citation II/SP permits operation at

14,700 pounds maximum takeoff weight. Engine: two Pratt & Whitney of Canada JT15D-4B, 2500 lbs. static thrust; maximum takeoff weight: 14,700 pounds; maximum speed: Vmo: 275 KIAS (29,300 feet); Mmo: 0.720 Mach (29,300 feet); wingspan: 52.2 feet; maximum operating altitude: 43,000 feet.

Cessna Citation III instrument panel.

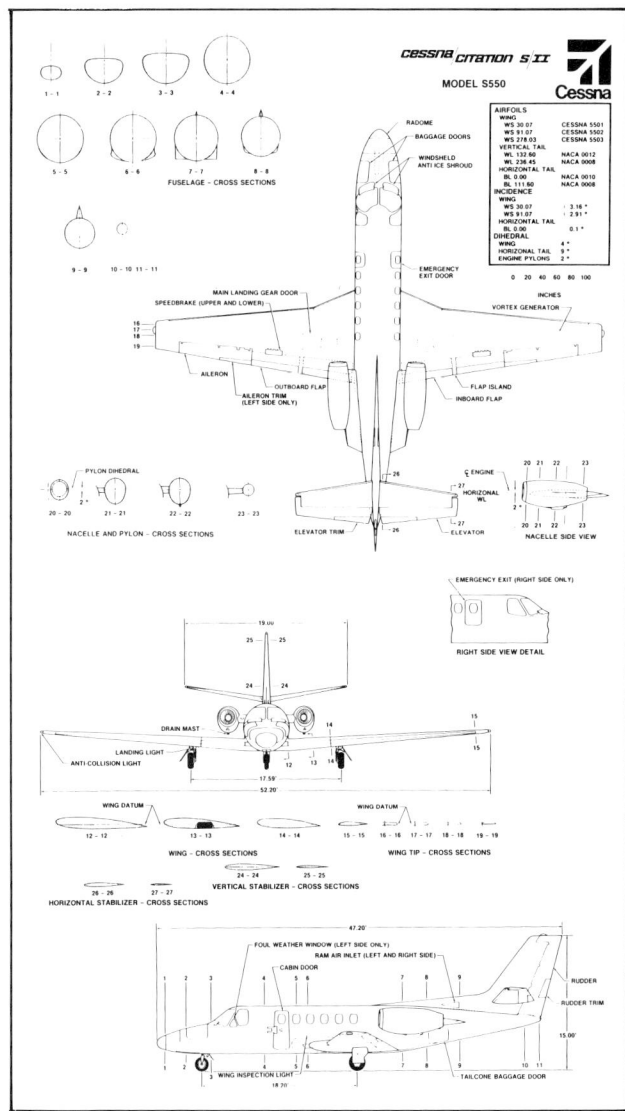

▼ MODEL S550/T-47A ATC A22CE 1984

Cessna won a contract with the U.S. Navy to modify 15 Model S550 Citation II jets for training RIO (Radar Intercept Operator) under the navy's Undergraduate Navy Flight Officer/Training System Upgrade program, replacing North American Rockwell T-39D aircraft. Cessna provides pilots (through screening by subcontractor Northrop), maintenance personnel and the special on-board Singer-Link radar simulators. Special changes include: wing span reduced to 46.5 feet and boosted ailerons to increase roll rate, high impact-resistant polycarbonate windshield (bird-tested) for 350-knot low level flights. Working in pairs, one T-47A acts as a bogey while the other is vectored into attack position by radar intercept operator trainees. Engine: two Pratt & Whitney of Canada JT15D-5, 2900 lbs. static thrust; maximum takeoff weight: 15,000 pounds; maximum speed: Vmo (sea level): 358 KIAS; Mmo: 0.750 Mach indicated (above 27,425 feet); wingspan: 47 feet; maximum operating altitude: 43,000 feet.

▲   MODEL 650   ATC A9NM   1979

After establishing the Citation I/II jets as worldwide leaders in jet sales, Cessna developed the Model 700 in a 1975 project proposal, featuring three turbofan engines and a supercritical, swept wing. An all-new design, the mid-size jet was redesigned with two engines, redesignated Model 650 and the prototype (c/n 696, N650CC) took off at 9:19 A.M. on May 30, 1979 with pilots Robert Leonard and Ellis Brady at the controls. The 25-degree swept wing uses spoilers for roll control and as speed brakes. Hydraulically-operated landing gear and power steering is standard. Two TFE-731 turbofans with thrust reversers power the Citation III. Pressurization system features 9.3 psi differential permitting an 8000-foot cabin at 51,000 feet. Certification was under FAR Part 25. First customer deliveries began in 1983 with golfer Arnold Palmer receiving the first production airplane, later registered as N1AP. Total sold (as of 12-31-84): 1983: 18; 1984: 50. Price (typically-equipped): $6,120,000 (1983). Engine: two Garrett TFE-731-3B-100S turbofans, 3650 lbs. static thrust; maximum takeoff weight: 21,000 pounds, maximum landing weight: 17,000 pounds; maximum speed: Vmo: 293 KIAS (34,275 feet); Mmo: 0.851 Mach indicated (34,275 feet); wingspan: 53.5 feet; maximum operating altitude: 51,000 feet. As of 1986, 102 Citation III airplanes were operating worldwide.

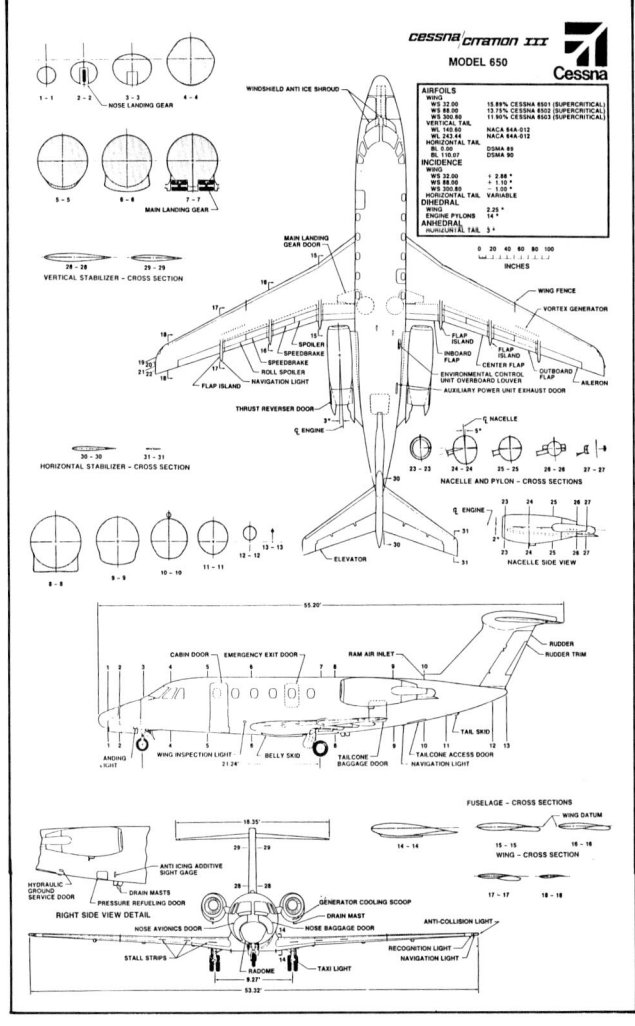

MODEL 620 EXPERIMENTAL 1956

Cessna took a bold step forward in 1954 when it announced a pressurized, eight-to-10 seat business airplane powered by four engines that was intended to replace many aging postwar aircraft serving as executive transportation. In September, 1953 Ralph Harmon was assigned the task of designing the airplane, known only as the Model 620. First flight was made on Saturday, August 11, 1956 from McConnell Air Force Base with Dale Westfall pilot, and Bill Stinson, co-pilot. Features of the Model 620 included: on-board APU (auxiliary power unit), air conditioning system, four 350 hp geared, supercharged Continental opposed engines with three-blade constant-speed, full-feathering propellers. Over 400 gallons of fuel was carried in the wings/tip tanks and the airplane had a six-foot high, stand-up cabin. After more than 50 hours of flight testing, Cessna decided not to produce the Model 620, one reason being a ready supply of large, pressurized airliners available at an economical price. The airplane was eventually sold for scrap. Total built: one (c/n 620, N620E). Price (estimated): $375,000. Engine: four Continental GSO-526-A, 350 hp; gross takeoff weight: 13,650 pounds, maximum landing weight: 13,000 pounds; maximum speed: 282 mph (15,000 feet); wingspan: 55 feet; service ceiling: 27,500 feet; three-engine service ceiling: 22,500 feet. Color: Brilliant two-tone green and white.

▲ MODEL 1014/1034 XMC EXPERIMENTAL   1971-72
Designed for testing of advanced aerodynamic/materials concepts, Cessna's XMC (Experimental Magic Carpet) placed the pilot ahead of the swept-back, full-cantilever wing with the 100 hp engine mounted behind a two-place cabin. First flown in January, 1971, the XMC completed all Phase I flight tests consisting of flying, ground handling characteristics and visibility in the flight regime then entered Phase II testing in May, 1971. The second evaluation period tested methods that could be employed to reduce weight and cost of both single and multi-engine Cessna airplanes. A shroud was installed around the propeller in 1972, the spatted nose gear was redesigned with a wheel fairing, vertical stabilizer area was increased, wing tips revised and the designation was changed to Model 1034 but still called the XMC. Other experiments with CG effects, control surface location/response, cabin noise levels and relationship of wing to engine/propeller were tested. Total built: one (c/n 674, N7174C). Engine: Continental O-200A, 100 hp; wingspan: 32 feet. Model 1034 is illustrated. Model 1014 first flight: 1-22-71; pilot: Bruce Barrett; Model 1034 first flight: 6-1-72; pilot: Bruce Barrett

▲ MODEL CH-1C SKYHOOK   ATC 3H10   1961-62

Charles Siebel developed his S-4B helicopter after starting Seibel Helicopter Company, located in Wichita, in 1947. Cessna purchased the company in 1952 and hired Siebel as chief helicopter engineer. A two-place rotorcraft was designed with the 260 hp, turbocharged powerplant ahead of the crew compartment. Designated Cessna CH-1 (c/n 45001, N5155), it first flew in 1954 and received its ATC in June, 1955. Next came the CH-1A, a four-place ship rebuilt from the original CH-1 and powered by a 260 hp engine (c/n 45002) that was quickly followed by the CH-1B (c/n 45004). Cessna offered a commercial model, the CH-1C Skyhook powered by a 270 hp, supercharged powerplant. The CH-1C was very stable in flight, becoming first known helicopter to receive FAA approval for operations in IFR weather. Deliveries began in 1961 but production was terminated by 1963 because of declining sales. Total built: CH-1C: 29 (including 6 YH-41 repurchased from the U.S. Army and rebuilt as CH-1C). Price: $79,960 (1961). Engine: Continental FSO-526-A, 270 hp with supercharging; gross weight: 3100 pounds; maximum speed: 122 mph; rotor diameter: 35 feet; hovering ceiling: 9600 feet. A CH-1C is illustrated.

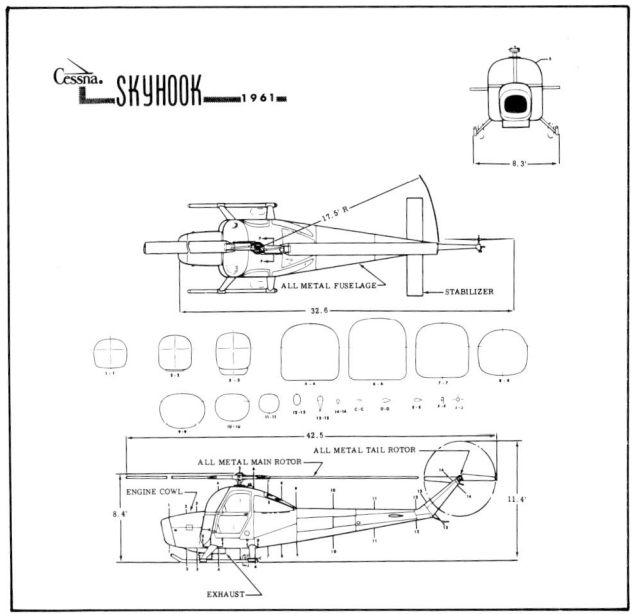

MODEL YH-41 (CH-1B)   ATC 3H10   1957 ▶

United States Army interest in Cessna's helicopter resulted in an evaluation order for 10 aircraft in 1957, designated as YH-41 "Seneca." Deliveries began in late 1957 and were completed in June, 1958. Under the Military Assistance Program, the army procured five YH-41 for Iran and the air force purchased six for Ecuador. In 1958 a member of the army's Aviation Board piloted a YH-41 to almost 30,000 feet above Wichita, setting three world records. Total built: 11. Engine: Continental FSO-526-A (forward-mounted), 270 hp with supercharging; gross weight: 3100 pounds; maximum speed: 122 mph; rotor diameter: 35 feet; hovering ceiling: 9600 feet. CH-1B military demonstrator (YH-41) is illustrated. Note streamlined nose cowl around engine, vertical rotor control shaft inside the cabin. (Reference Appendix A, #31)

APPENDIX A FOOTNOTES

Note: Constructor numbers listed in these footnotes are from official Cessna Aircraft Company publications and indicate c/n blocks assigned to a model year of aircraft but do not necessarily reflect total production during a model year.

1. First Reims-built Model 150 was the 1966 F150F. 67 airplanes were produced. Constructor numbers were: c/n F15000001 to F15000067; 1967 F150G: c/n F15000068 to F15000219; 1968 F150H: c/n F15000220 to F15000389; 1969 F150J: c/n F15000390 to F15000529. Domestic c/n were: 1966 150F: 15061533 to 15064532; 1967 150G: 15064533 to 15067198; 1968 150H: 15067199 to 15069308; 1969 150J: 15069309 to 15071128.

2. Reims also built the F150K in 1970. Constuctor numbers were: 1970 F150K: c/n F15000530 to F15000658; 1970 FA150K Aerobat: c/n FA1500001 to FA15000081. In 1970 Model 150 production returned to the Wichita facility after two years (1968-69) of manufacture at Cessna's Winfield, Kansas factory. Domestic c/n were: 1970 150K: 15071129 to 15072003.

3. 1971-73 Reims F150L constructor numbers were: c/n F15000659 to F15001013; FA150L Aerobat: c/n FA1500082 to FA1500120, FRA1500121 to FRA1500211. Domestic c/n were: 1971 150L: 15072004 to 15072628; 1972 150L: 15072629 to 15073658; 1973 150L: 15073659 to 15074850.

4. 1974-77 Reims F15001014 to F15001428; FRA150L Aerobat: c/n FRA1500212 to FRA1500336. As of 12-31-84, Cessna had built 22,082 Model 150 while Reims had produced 1758. Production returned to Strother Field from 1973-77, with 8300 Model 150 produced there during 1968-69/1973-77.

5. 1978-80 Reims constructor numbers were: F15201429 to F15201808; FA152: FA1520337 to FA1520372. Domestic c/n were: 1978 152: 15279406 to 15282031; 1979 152: 15282032 to 15283591; 1980 152: 15283592 to 15284541.

6. 1978-82 Reims FA152 constructor numbers were: 1978: FA1520337 to FA1520347; 1979: FA1520348 to FA1520357; 1980: FA1520358 to FA1520372; 1981: FA1520373 to FA1520377; 1982: FA1520378 to FA1520382. Domestic: A1520735 to A1520808; 1979: A1520809 to A1520878; 1980: A1520879 to A1520943; 1981: A1520944 to A1520983; 1982: A1520984 to A1521014.

7. 1981-85 Reims F152 constructor numbers were: 1981: F15201819 to F15201893; 1982: F15201894 to F15201928; 1983: F15201929 to F15201943; 1984: F15201944 to F15201952; 1985: F15201953 to F15201965. Domestic: 1981: 15284542 to 15285161; 1982: 15285162 to 15285594; 1983: 15285595 to 15285833; 1984: 15285834 to 15285939; 1985: 15285940 to 15286033.

8. The last 1952 production Model 170B, c/n 25372 exported to New Zealand, registered ZK-AZC to Rural Aviation Ltd. while the first 1956 production Model 170B, c/n 26996 was exported to Costa Rica as TI-247. Last 1955 production Model 170B, c/n 26995 was exported to Phnom Penh, Cambodia and the final production 1956 Model 170B, c/n 27169 was exported to Argentina with the temporary registration of LV-PDH.

9. 18 1963 P172D were manufactured in Wichita, disassembled, crated and shipped to Reims, assigned Reims c/n F17200001 to F17200018, reassembled and sold.

10. Three 1963 P172D Skyhawk Powermatic were shipped to Reims as FP172. The last P172D assembled by Reims, c/n P17257189, N8589X became R172H, N1909F with same c/n but equipped with a Continental IO-360-D, 210 hp.

11. Of the 67 1964 Model F172E built by Reims, 41 airplanes originally received Wichita constructor numbers. They were: F17200019 to F17200085. Model 172J was original designation for what eventually became the Model 177/Cardinal and was not assigned to 172/Skyhawk series.

12. Reims F172K to F172M production was: 1969-70 F172K: 50; 1971-72 F172L: 100; 1973-75 F172M: 480; 1976 F172M: 130. Reims also built the FR172H/J from 1971-76 with 210 hp Continental IO-360-D and called the Reims Rocket.

13. Reims FR172K (Reims Rocket) production, 1977-81: c/n FR17200591 to FR17200675 inclusive.

14. USAF T-41A serial numbers were: 65-5100 to 65-5269. T-41A c/n were scattered throughout c/n block 17251947 to 17253392.

15. U.S. Army T-41B serial numbers were: 67-15000 to 67-15254; T-41B c/n were scattered throughout c/n block R172-0001 to R1720255 (including R1720256, the prototype Reims Rocket with Reims c/n FR172E0001).

16. USAF T-41C serial numbers were: 68-7866 to 68-7910; 69-7750 to 69-7756. T-41C c/n were scattered throughout c/n block R172-0257 to R172-0301, R172-0426 to R172-0432.

17. Cessna built 299 T-41D, c/n R172-0302 to R172-0608 (except for USAF T-41C, c/n block R172-0426 to R172-0432 and experimental c/n 559 that was Model 172J prototype). Of 299 built, 94 were delivered to foreign governments under the Military Assistance Program as follows: Peru (40); Colombia (30); Ecuador (14); Honduras (5); Argentina (3); Isreal (2). According to official Cessna publications, as of 12-31-84, 320 T-41D had been built since 1968.

18. 20 F177RG were built by Reims in 1972: c/n F177RG0043 to F177RG0062; 30 F177RG were built in 1973: c/n F177RG0063 to F177RG0092. 30 F177RG were built in 1974: c/n F177RG0093 to F177RG0122; 16 F177RG were built in 1975: c/n F177RG0123 to F177RG0138. 22 F177RG were built in 1976: c/n F177RG0139 to F177RG0160; 16 F177RG were built in 1977: c/n F177RG0161 to F177RG0177.

19. 17 U-17C (Model 180 E and H) c/n were: 1962: 18051134, 18051143, 18051145, 18051147, 18051149, 18051151, 18051153, 18051155; 1966: 18051649, 18051653, 18051687 (USAF s/n 65-12771, 65-12770 and 67-14602); 1967: 18051795, 18051796, 18051851 (USAF s/n 67-14580, 67-14581, 67-14603); 1970: 18052145, 18052172, 18052174 (USAF s/n 70-1624, 70-2034, 70-2035).

20. Four 1961 Model 182D (Canadian National Defense L-19L) CDN s/n were: 16726, 16727, 16728, 16729.

21. Argentine 1967 A182K c/n were: A182-0057 to A182-0096. 20 1968 A182L c/n were: A182-0097 to A182-0116. 20 1972 A182 c/n were: A182-0117 to A182-0136, all built in 1972 model year.

22. 1963 U-17A scattered throughout c/n block 185-0513 to 185-0653; 1964 U-17A scattered throughout c/n block 185-0654 to 185-0776; 1965-67 U-17A scattered throughout c/n block 185-0777 to 185-1300.

23. 1967-73 U-17B scattered throughout c/n block 185-1150 to 185-02310.

24. Official Cessna records indicate that no further c/n have been assigned for the ag-series airplanes since 1983. Colombia built 87 Agwagon/Agtruck between 1972-75. 24 AGpickup/AGwagon were assembled in Argentina between 1972-73.

25. It is interesting to note that in 1946 Cessna applied for an Approved Type Certificate for an economy version of the Model 190 to be called the Model 170 with 145 hp Warner Super Scarab radial engine, but withdrew the request in favor of reserving the 170 number for future use.

26. The most common powerplants were: Jacobs L4MB, 225-245 hp; Jacobs R-755-A2 and -9 (required seven minor modifications for installation) and Continental W-670 engines above serial

number 90000-23 (W 670 engines below this s/n were not eligible for Cessna factory installation under the CAA change). After January, 1952 the only customer-supplied engines that could be factory installed were the Jacobs L4MB or R-755-9. The Model 195B was powered by a remanufactured Jacobs R-755-B2 incorporating many improvements found in the 245 hp Jacobs R-755-9. First deliveries of the 195B were scheduled for spring, 1952. One particular 1948 Model 195 that came up for sale was the personal mount of Cessna President Dwane L. Wallace. With 250 hours total time, brown exterior paint trim and loaded with Sperry gyro instruments and Lear avionics, the price tag was $16,294.

27. USAF LC-126A serial numbers were: 49-1947 through 49-1960. National Guard LC-126B serial numbers were: 50-1250 through 50-1252, 50-1255 through 50-1271 (possibly 50-1291, Cessna records uncertain). U.S. Army LC-126C serial numbers were: 51-6958 through 51-7018, 52-6314 and 52-6315.

28. In 1985 Cessna sold manufacturing rights and the Approved Type Certificate for the Model 305 to Regal Air, Mt. Pleasant, Texas.

29. Model 305/L-19 production breakdown is:

MODEL	DESIGNATION	C/N BLOCKS	NUMBER BUILT
305	Prototype	N/A	1
305A	L-19 - O-1A	50-1327 - 50-1744	418
		51-4534 - 51-5109	576
		51-7286 - 51-7481	196
		51-11912 - 51-12911	1002 (1)
		51-16864 - 51-16973	110
		53-2873 - 53-2878	6 (To Chile)
		53-7698 - 53-7717	20
		53-7968 - 53-8067	100 (16 Canada)
	OE-1 - O-1B	BuAer 133782 - 133816	35 (USMC)
		BuAer 136887 - 136911	25 (USMC)
		BuAer 144663 - 144664	2 (USMC)
		N1170D - N1173D	4 (Civil)
	XL-19B	52-1804	1
	XL-19C	52-6311 - 52-6312	2
305B	TL-19D - TO-1D	55-4649 - 55-4748	100
		57-2772 - 57-2981	210
305C	L-19E - O-1E	56-2467 - 56-2696	230
		56-4034 - 56-4038	5 (To Canada)
		56-4161 - 56-4172	12
		56-4175 - 56-4235	61
		57-1606 - 57-1609	4 (To Canada)
		57-5983 - 57-6028	46
		57-6268 - 57-6277	10
		French Army/Air Force	126
		61-2955 - 61-3024	70
		61-12280 - 62-12288	9
		151776 - 151779	4 (U.S. Navy)
		63-12745 - 63-12758	14
		TOTAL BUILT: 3399 (2)	

(1) Air Force s/n 51-12671 and 51-12672 destroyed by storm before delivery. Two additional airplanes with same s/n built as replacements.
(2) Total does not include airplanes built under license in Japan or the Model 321 (OE-2).

30. Cessna proposed to build a commercial, four-place version of the Model 318 known as the Model 407, but the project never progressed beyond the 1959 mockup stage.

31. The versatile Citation II can compete in price directly with the Beechcraft Model B200 and Model 300 Super King Air executive turboprops, making it a popular choice among companies stepping up to turbine-powered equipment for the first time. First Citation II was c/n 595.

32. U.S. Army YH-41 constructor numbers were: 45005 through 45014, army s/n 56-4236 through 56-4245. Military Assistance Program CH-1C c/n and allocated FAA registration numbers were: Shipped to Iran: c/n 45515 (N5715), 45517 (N5717), 45519 (N5719), 45521 (N5721), 45528 (N5728). Shipped to Ecuador: c/n 45522, 45523, 45524, 45525, 45526 (N5726), 45529 (N5729). Only one YH-41 is known to exist, s/n 56-4244, Cessna c/n 45013, displayed at the U.S. Army Aviation Museum at Fort Rucker, Alabama.

INDEX

MODEL	PAGE	MODEL	PAGE	MODEL	PAGE
120	6	182F-Q	34	308-309	55
140	6-7	182M	34	310-310C	56
140A	8	182R	35	310D-G	57
150	9	T182R	35	310H-N	58
150A-C	9	R/R182	35	310P-R	59
150D-K	9	185-185D	37	310R	60
A150K/L	10	A185E	37	U-3A/B	60
150L/M	11	A185E/F	38	A/T-37	61
152	12	U-17A	38	319/320	62
A152	12	U-17B	39	320A-F	63
160	13	187	39	321	64
170	14	188/A188	40	325	64
170A	14	A188A	41	335	64
170A/B	15	188B	41	377/327	65
172	16	A188B	41	336	65
172A-I	17	T188C	41	337/T337	66
P172D	17	190	42	337-P337	67
172K-P	18	195/A/B	43	O-2A/B	68
172Q	19	LC-126	43	340/340A	69
R172K	19	X-210	43	401-401B	70
172RG	20	205	44	402-402B	71
T-41A/B	21	206	44	402B/C	72
T-41C/D	22	U/TU206	44	404	73
175	23	P206B	45	F406	73
175A/B	23	U206E/G	45	411	74
175C	24	TU206E/G	45	411A	74
177	25	207/T207	46	414	75
177A/B	25	STATIONAIR 7	47	414A	76
177B	26	T207 (export)	47	421	77
177B	27	208/A/B	48	421A	77
177RG	27	U-27A	48	421B/C	78
180	28	210	49	425	79
180A-F	28	210A-F	50	441	80
180G-H	29	210G-N	51	500/501	81
180J-K	30	210N/R	52	550/551	82
U-17C	30	P210N/R	52	S550	83
182	32	303/T303	53	650	84
182A/B	32	305	54	620	85
182C-E	33	L-19	55	1014/34	86
L-19L	33	XL-19B/C	55	CH-1	87

1961 Model 185 equipped with floats. Note how the airplane's paint scheme has been carried over to the floats. ▲

Sky King (Kirby Grant) and Penny (Gloria Winters) pose for the camera with Songbird III, a 1960 Model 310D, N6817T (c/n 39117). ▲

Factory-fresh Model 185 Skywagons await delivery to the Government of Peru. All nine ships have the optional cargo pack. ▼

1965 Model 182H was purchased by the Argentina Ministry of Defense for general liaison duties. ▲

T-41D (R172H) for Ecuador shows long dorsal fin and spring steel main gear struts common to all T-41D airplanes. ▲

Original configuration of the Model 1014 XMC shows spatted nose gear and unshrouded propeller. ▲

1975 Model A188B AgWagon taxies out for another sortie against insect-infested crops. ▼

Interesting view of the prototype Model 210. Note unusual location of registration number on wing. ▲

1954 Model 180 for the Mexican Navy. Note low mounting position for name "Cessna," high mounting of 'bird' logo on tail. ▼

Experimental O-2T featured two Allison 250 gas turbine engines. First flight was 1967.

Model TU206G was sold to Venezuela in 1982. Note special camouflage pattern. N9748Z is c/n U20606642.

Combat-ready O-2A rests at Khe Sahn base, Republic of Vietnam. Note kangaroo and tip stripes on vertical stabilizers.

A pair of U-17s fly reconnaisance patrol over ricefields of the Ca Mau peninsula, Republic of Vietnam.

Maintenance crew works on A-37A in revetment at Bien Hoa Air Base, Republic of Vietnam.

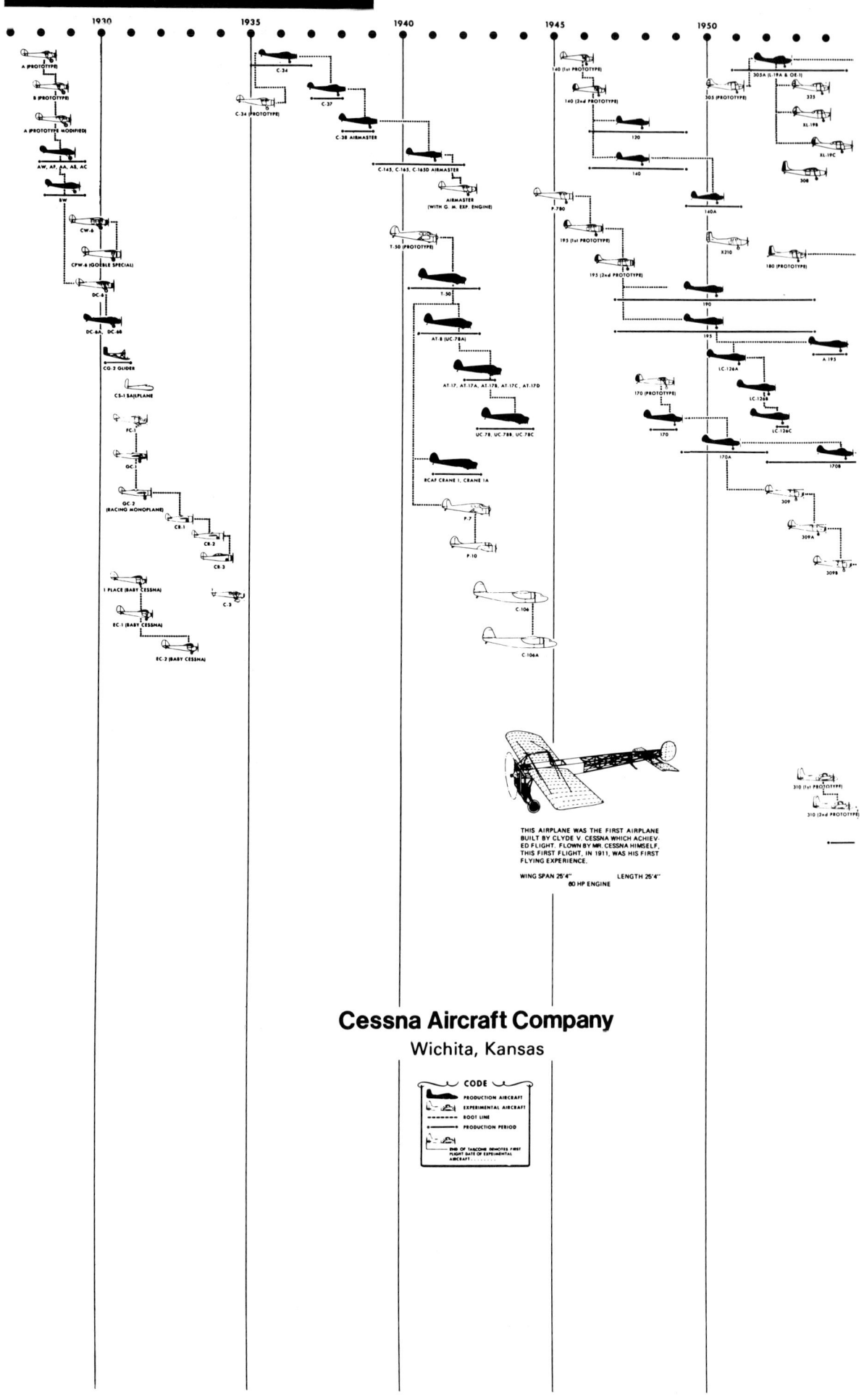

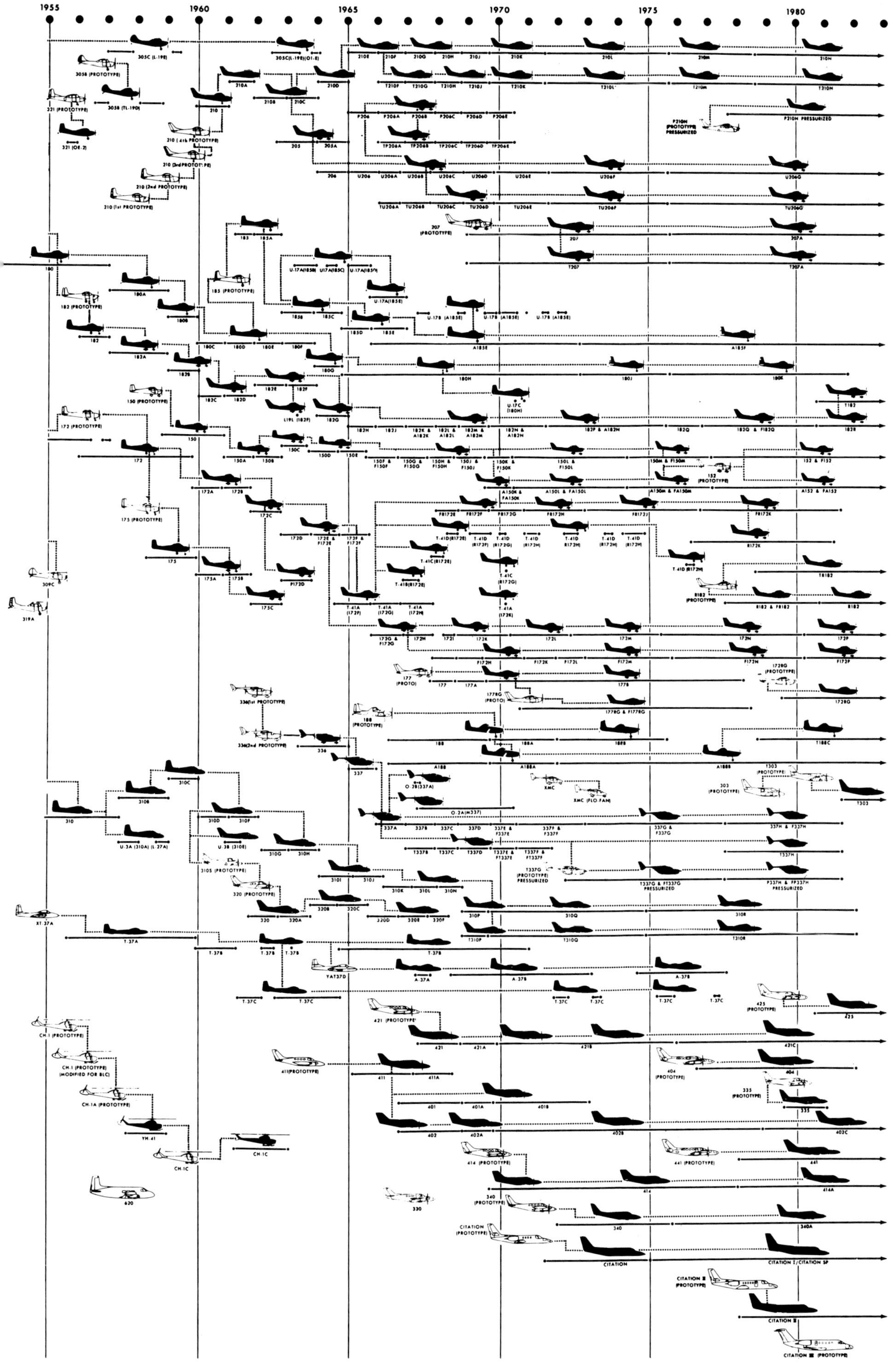